# WHITE LIES (for my mother)

# WHITE
# LIES
## *(for my mother)*

## Liza Potvin

NeWest Press • Edmonton

*Canadian Cataloguing in Publication Data*
Potvin, Elizabeth Ann, 1958 -
White Lies (for my mother)

   ISBN 0-920897-13-4
   1. Potvin, Elizabeth Ann, 1958 -      2.
Incest victims--Canada--Biography. I. Title.
HQ72.C3P68 1992   306.877'092    C92-091146-3

*Credits*
Cover design:  Diane Jensen
Interior design:  Diane Jensen
Editor for the Press:  Smaro Kamboureli

Financial Assistance:  NeWest Press gratefully acknowledges
the financial assistance of Alberta Culture and Multiculturalism,
The Alberta Foundation for the Arts, The Canada Council, and
The NeWest Institute for Western Canadian Studies.

The writer gratefully acknowledges the assistance of
The Canada Council in completing this project.

Printed and Bound in Canada by Best Gagné Book Manufacturers.

NeWest Publishers Limited
#310, 10359-82 Avenue
Edmonton, Alberta
T6E 1Z9

Dedicated, with love, to all those women who have mothered me.


(Especially: Malka Kaufman, Deborah Hudson, Maroussia Ahmed,
Rose Cope, Ana Coutinho, Vera Finnich, Glennis Stephenson,
Pia Kolbe, Lyn Shulha, Maria Forte and Joan Coldwell.)


And to the one who could not.


Special thanks to Sheila Watson, David Helwig, Steve Guppy, Ron
Smith, Brenda Sully, Carol Matthews, and Kathryn Barnwell for
reading earlier drafts and making recommendations. I am indebted
to Carol Matthews for her insight on *The Wizard of Oz* , and to Smaro
Kamboureli for editorial suggestions.

I speak with the voice of Philomela, of silence and of pain. Which is to say I do not speak at all. The blankness of the page is my message that invites your gaze, your speculation. I have woven my secrets into the white spaces of nothingness, from rags once torn and then bonded together, waiting for you to unravel them. I could write nothing at all, and you would know just what it is I am saying. *Mais il faut m'aider.*

Maman, I think of you and your silences, and I know that I can no longer keep quiet. *Keep still. It won't hurt. If you have nothing good to say about anyone, better to say nothing at all. Wait to see what happens. Say your rosary beads, pray for guidance.* Why are we always waiting?

Maman, there is no one to rescue us now.  No prince will arrive when you flash your glittering S.O.S. with your pocketbook mirror, or scrawl your delicate messages in red lipstick across the mirror: MAYDAY.  And I am growing lonely in my meditations.  I am cold tonight.  I follow your thoughts, I speak to you quietly. *Je te suis.*  But you never answer me.  You are preoccupied, praying to your saviour.

I have a recurring dream in which I run through a field of scrub and daisies. The barn in the field looks familiar, as does the suburb springing up on the edge of the field like an untameable growth, a festering sore in the ground, where the cranes and plows move like giant vultures. All around me there are uprooted trees, torn and bleeding. I do not know the people who inhabit this prehistoric terrain. I enter a door that flies open in the wind. A woman sits in a rocking chair in the frame of a structure that promises to become a house one day, the cold sky lit blue behind the hardwood skeleton, hollow eye sockets in place of windows. Beyond the woman cumulus clouds billow like soft curls, making her face as old as the parched earth.

Do you live here? I ask.
*No,* she responds hesitantly.

At her feet lie sample books of ceramic bathroom tiles, knitted together in squares, linoleum scraps, carpet swatches, new paint cans, as if she had just consulted an interior designer and were now compelled to arrive at some decision. Her face wears an expression of complete bewilderment. As I come closer, I notice that she is doing handwork, her fingers wrapped around a wooden spool; a snake composed of coloured wool patches equal in length descends from the matrix of the spool. As she picks up each thread on her needle and lifts it onto the spikes on top of the spool, the coil grows longer and longer, spinning around on itself in spirals like a discarded orange peel.

*This is your connection to me.*

Who are you making this for?

*No one in particular.*

May I see it?

*It is not finished yet.*

The woman turns away, and begins writing a letter, but she does not let me see the page, keeps turning her back to me when I approach.

Each time I have the dream again, it ends with the dreaded sensation of my falling through the air after leaping from a cliff, but I never seem to land. My conversation with the woman varies slightly each time; occasionally, she refuses to speak to me at all. I am obsessed with this dream woman, who looks like no one I know. In my ongoing dialogue with her, she always terminates our conversation by uttering in an exasperated tone—

*What is it?*

In the evenings, you sit in your living room—what a strange name for a room where no one really lives—watching the coals glow in the fireplace, feigning contentment, realigning the books on the coffee table, nervously straightening the cushions on the sofa until they are just right, thinking—Order, Peace. I have made it through another day, thank God. Sitting in the cold empty splendour of the Snow Queen's palace.

And you feel lulled by that sense of completion, the evening news wraps it up for you, the gentle hum of the dishwasher upstairs as it goes through its last cycle. Listen carefully, Maman. A dull thud, a clunk, another thud, then whirr! A muted cry as the dishwasher whines toward its next phase. Remind yourself that you must call the repairman tomorrow. There it goes again—thunk! As if all that trapped porcelain and glass were banging against the walls to be released, fists pounding in incredulity against the belly of the Maytag whale, hitting over and over again. Thud, sigh. Thud, sigh. And every crackling snore from the fire log has the thin snap of fine leather whacking the air. The dog sleeping at the hearth, which dreams of nothing but hunting and eating, begins to whimper, its mouth quivering. Listen carefully to the rhythms of your suburban nights, Maman, when you feel protected from the whiteness of the snow falling heavily all around you. Insisting always on quality, you have paid dearly for such tranquility. Listen to the counterpoint to your rhythms, that nearly undetectable current, running just below the surface, as the machine comes to the end of its cycle. A small chant, not quite in harmony with the rest.

Maman, this is my song to you. This is our song. It is not a pretty song. Not one of those lovely classical melodies you wanted me to play for you on the piano to soothe your nerves, to assure you that your daughter would succeed where you never could, the rarefied celestial realms of music. My work, like my tongue, is cut out for me, so the lyrics are ragged. I bleed as I speak, red ink pouring across the page. But even if my voice falters, if my line is incoherent, remember that sorrow, like music, is inventive.

I saw Him once as you did. Lying here in this white bed, wrapped in layers of white sheets and Demerol, I waited for Him to arrive, like a bridegroom to a feast. He too was dressed in white, an ebony serpent with silver studs around his neck, richly decorated with titles. *Arise, my pale one, and come with me.* And yes, Maman, I followed Him. And He looked down at the thread of scarlet, a bright red seal upon my wrist, and said, *Do not worry, I will take care of you, my innocent dove.* And I believed Him. Although He vanished like a Ghost, I believed Him.

8

So many lies, Maman. So many times I have tried to lie still, here among the white sheets. But always there are stains, traces of former lives, like the bleeding Sacred Heart hanging over my bed, dripping down methodically on my forehead in the middle of the night, destroying the whiteness of the sheets. This image returns to me in moments of terror, even now. The priest explains to us that we are all born with a white soul, unblemished. To sin is to blacken the soul, an indelible muddy mark, a gradually accumulated patchwork of past errors visible only to God and the sinner. I envision a dirty lung, choking on its own filth, making it harder for me to breathe; it is the image most easily summoned from my memory, instant and precise as a dagger, starkly painted in black and white. In health class, a nurse, one of the girls' mothers, shows us a picture of a smoker's lung, a loathsome x-ray that will stay with me forever because I believe it is intended as His personal reminder of my sinfulness. I lie in bed at night, wondering how I will ever erase all this blackness inside me, how will He forgive me my trespasses? Soon there will be no more white spaces, and I will be lost to the place of flames.

*Do not tell your mother. It would kill her. She already has so many problems because of you, you make her life so difficult. Just do what I tell you to and let her have some rest. A white lie is only venial, not as bad as a mortal lie. It is a mortal sin to tell black lies, do you hear me? But sometimes white lies are necessary. You will understand that someday.*

Are you really resting, Maman? At night, it is possible for me to hear you behind the closed bathroom door, retching into the toilet bowl. The bathroom is across the hallway, whereas the room where you lie resting is directly adjoined to my bedroom. Can you really hear nothing through the paper thin walls that separate us?

I lie here thinking of you, and my heart trembles; I cannot sleep; I ache for you. But I have been a bad girl, and do not deserve the fragrant touch of your palm across my forehead to cleanse away the sins of the world. Lot and daughter lick the salt wounds of the world. What I want is unqualified love, universal acceptance. I dream of the coolness of holy water from the water font beside my bedroom door, the benign face of the Blessed Virgin veiled by its plastic Woolworth frame. But I cannot move toward it; I am sore; I am sorry. *Forgive me, Father, for I have sinned.* The only time He is ever gentle with me. God the Father, and my Father, what is the difference? Both of them want to save my soul. Both of them do nothing when I pray for it to stop.

*Stupid fucking girl. You are so ugly no one wants to look at you. How will I ever get someone to marry you, when you are so ugly and clumsy and have no brains? If you keep biting your nails, you will be punished. This is for nothing, take off your pants, imagine what you will get if you really do something! That's funny. Tabernacle! You are supposed to laugh, you stupid bitch. Don't you ever listen to me? Maudite femme, you have your mother's cold blood in your veins.*

Where do I begin? There never was a beginning; it always happened, as long as I can remember. My ordinary life is only the lit room, the visible surface, of the real and mysterious life which is the other place where I dwell. More and more I sense that my ordinary life is extraneous, irrelevant, that the precarious balancing act I have always maintained between those twin lives is shifting. The cracks are widening, the centre of gravity has moved to an unknown place. There are no walls in this other world. I wake from my dreams of it startled, shaken, with the sensation of falling forever through space, no solid ground beneath me, no easy landing. No memories, only vague pictures to cling to, clues to a previous existence shaped by distant voices, apparitions, premonitions. My days pass in a fog of disbelief and disenchantment with my ordinary life; something is missing; it is too unreal. I move slowly from room to room, cleaning and organizing, discarding and saving according to some inner whim. I remake my clothes from garments I have long outgrown, seduced by the rich textures of these old fabrics, but not understanding their history, their secrets. I am waiting; I am watching; my body is changing shape. I try on every outfit in my closet, blend summer cottons with winter woolens to test for effects, searching for whatever might emerge, some clue, the slightest hint of who I might really be, intimations of some other season just beyond the impenetrable wall. There are no assurances, no guarantees on the other side of the closet, just this fanatic obsession with organizing and segregating the world of my dreams, storing the rest in mothballs, the disguise of conformity. My room is littered with the debris of normality, smashed and robbed. I think there are children on the other side of the wall; I hear conspiratorial whispers and giggles; one young child in particular is always laughing at me. My external world ceases to function; there are no words left. I think I may be going mad.

Humpty Dumpty sat on a wall.
Humpty Dumpty had a great fall.
All the Queen's horses and all the Queen's men
Couldn't put her together again.

In the beginning there was a white bed, the tousled linen *from which the Lord has arisen.* And I am back in the white bed now, watching and waiting. Four months ago, my daughter was born and swaddled in identical white sheets, and now I am back here. I am watching my partner change her diaper, when a voice inside me, as young as the one behind the closet wall, screams *Stop! Leave her alone!* My hysteria continues for hours. I have a picture of Him again, standing over the creche of my little sister, masturbating as He holds her little body still, the semen soaking into her flannel diaper. I feel nauseous; hot tears of rage choke my words; my jaw clenches and my anger burns a hole inside me. A man in white decides that I cannot be a good mother right now, that I need to get better first. But what I want most is her soft little body next to mine, the promise of protection provided. What have they done with her?

And then the thread of scarlet, trickling down my arm. The voice that insists that I am no good, a lousy mother. *You are stupid, you are bad, you forget things, you make up lies.* But I had to do it. Just a white lie. I had no choice.

The man in white is tired of me. I can tell. Nothing I do pleases Him anymore, I do not tell Him what He needs to know. I have lost the magic formula. I look ugly in institutional blue. There is a little girl inside my head who talks back to Him while my outer voice remains mute. He has no time to listen to me, because she keeps interrupting me and saying that everything is fine. She sends me memory pictures, expects me to fit them together like still frames blending into continuous film. She confuses me. I want her to go away. She contradicts herself. *Let me contradict myself.* I get all muddled; the lies come back, and He says I am not making sense anymore. He gives me this notebook to write it out when it comes back to me. *Get the story straight.* I must remember all my dreams, write everything I can remember about my childhood. That should take one page, I tell Him. Just an exercise. No sequences, no patterns. *Easier for both of us.*

Here in the ward I am convinced I am in grade two again, seeking translucent blue stickers of the Virgin Mary for my exercise book, for perfect penmanship. The blank page stares at me, sanctified by the initials J.M.J. in the upper right hand corner. Now I have nothing else to do but to stare at these blank whitewashed walls, the bars along the windows casting slim shadows across the linoleum. When the sun hurts my eyes, I look at the notebook and the lines repeat themselves across my page. From nine to eleven, and again from two to four, I have the pen, under supervision. In case I try to use it against myself. No razor. My legs sprout hair, the stubble scraping against the starched linen. The nurse will help me with my bath afterwards. Only do not let her touch me. I could not bear that, after all these years of waiting for your touch, Maman. Always I am waiting for you, Maman.

In the beginning no words appear; there are no words to convey the truth, only feelings, disconnected and vague. Whole words, let alone sentences, refuse to come. Only an incoherent chant, grunts of preverbal pain. How I wish you were here, Maman, because only you can provide the conjunctive verbs, link these monosyllabic utterances with meaning. Animal words. Small. Ugly. Cry. Baby. Black. Mouth. Sin. Hole. Then He said I was to imagine writing to someone, a stranger even. That was when I thought of you, Maman.

There are no colours here; they must have removed them because they thought they were dangerous too. Everything is white or black, even the food, tasteless; the centres of hardboiled eggs are blackened, so I eat only the whites.

Where do I begin? *When I was a child, I spake as a child, I thought and I understood as a child. But when I became a woman, I put away childish things, and began to see through a glass darkly.* I wrapped all the dirty memories in darkness and stored them below the surface of my pale skin.

I open my vein to speak to you, Maman, to let it flow, to relieve the pain, and still you do not respond. Did you ever love me? Wasn't I lovable enough? When I re-emerge from these depths, will you be waiting there for me? In my brooding passion, I imagine that you come to rescue me, now an aged but wiser woman. Then I weep bitter tears, knowing you will never come back to me.

And I was so happy. I thought I was on my way home.

I have never understood why people study yoga, spend hours seeking release from the body. It has always seemed fundamentally simple; I can leave my body whenever I want to. It is never a religious experience for me. I thought everyone did this; nothing unusual; like going to sleep at night, shifting gears while driving, or lowering your voice when you want no one to hear you. I let my mind hover near the ceiling and watch my numbed body lying on the bed, limp, helpless and stupid while I float above it, a flying spectator. I have always looked at myself this way. In New Delhi I watched the fakirs sleep on nails to induce detachment, while I alone among the watchers remained unimpressed. After all, it is normal to feel nothing, watch passively while things happen to your outer body, as if they are happening to someone else. My body is not really mine. It only looks like me. Maybe I am just luckier than most; nothing can really touch me.

Except Chopin. One night my friends and I stumbled home late from a party, the narrow streets echoing with our footsteps and drunken laughter. From a balcony above us drifted the slow notes of Chopin's eternally mournful, falsely exuberant, tenth opus. I stopped dead. The piercing strains of that music thawed my winter mask: the thrilling swell of the crescendo, followed by the inevitable letdown, terrible sadness. Everyone looked at me, asked me what was wrong. Their gaiety and silliness seemed a sacrilege, incongruous with the sweet music in the air. I took a taxi, fuelled by tears and the sickness that comes after the release of too much repressed laughter, like a dull pain, foreshadow of a hangover. I rocked myself from side to side on the greasy upholstery of the back seat, moaning the same melody over and over again to myself. It was our song, Maman, the lullaby you once sang to rock me to sleep, painfully nostalgic. How I hate it. I hate everything.

Except oranges. The smell of a freshly-peeled orange pricks the air with the perfume of regret, stings my nose with memory. Oranges are sentimental to you, Maman, Christmas ornaments to be contemplated reverently in the palm of your hand before you permit yourself the privilege of consuming one. During the war your mother, a young girl at the time, smelled her first orange in a theater and asked her mother to identify that extraordinary odour. Six years later she tasted her first orange, a ceremony she reenacted each time she presented you with the fruit of her hard labour, more priceless than jewels. You learn this precious ritual of eating an orange from her. With your sparing and cautious gestures, you tease off the rind for me, present me with only a section of the fruit at a time, savouring every burst of juice. A feast of textures permeates this memory, forgotten stories of luxury, the colour of appreciation. No other smell can move my heart.

Except *Carven ma griffe.* A scent that tears me apart with its sweetness. The special way you smell as you lean over me where I sit reading my detective story, kiss me goodnight perfunctorily, barely masking your pleasure and excitement at going out with Him. The merciless scent of you lingers in the air; it seems every woman I meet is wearing it now. Like perfume, too many things remind me of you these days. And you are the one person I most need to forget.

I remember only in black and white. Everything can be reduced to this; no distortions; it is simpler that way. One is either good, or bad, nothing in between. My soul is pitch black, my room is white, white pages stretch out before me, waiting for the stain of black ink. Where, as a child, I only saw in black and white, but I dreamed in colour, secretly indulging myself in all that I was denied. Sometimes colours try to seep into my body, but I do not allow them entrance. Maman, you gave Him permission to enter me, you said I had to respect Him, so how could I say bad things about Him? *And the Lord entered.* At night an ethereal black creature visits me, whisking a broom around the corner. She is comely, she comforts me somehow. The only person I can count on for regular appearances. Her smile brings an unnatural light to the dark room; she is the negative of the starched white nurse who rolls me on my side to change the sweat-soaked sheets every morning.

I have nightmares about polar bears, wake up terrified and trembling. They do not stalk me or touch me in any way. Rather it is their passive staring that haunts me; I am transfixed by the glare of their glassy, bloodshot eyes. I simply lie down, turn stiff and let them tear me to shreds with their claws, that rip at my stomach first, a slow and painful evisceration. I do not know if this nightmare means anything. It makes no sense to me.

w h i t e   l i e s   ( f o r   m y   m o t h e r )

You speak the language of the Snow Queen, syllables drip slowly from the icicles of your Nordic tongue. In your looking glass, the loveliest forest scenery appears like boiled spinach, while all that is good and beautiful shrinks into nothing. When you hold your mirror up, I can see that it is made of thousands of splinters, some even smaller than a grain of sand. If a little glass splinter becomes lodged in the heart, it is transformed into a lump of ice. Just like the Hans Christian Andersen tale you tell me over and over again. You belong to that northern country where nothing unfreezes, and you fly through the night in a black cloud. Not quite human. When you fly through the town in winter and peer in at the windows, they freeze into curious crystalline patterns that people mistake for flowers. No one can see in or out. Your eyes glitter like stars, but there is no peace or quiet in them.

*Do you feel cold? Creep into my bearskin.* And you put me beside you in your majestic snow sledge and wrap your furs around me. But it feels like sinking into a snowdrift, and I still shiver inwardly. You dazzle me with your beauty, but your kisses are colder than ice, they go straight to my heart. People say I am dead, my purple lips protruding. They do not see me wrapped up in your furs; they cannot know I dream of riding away with you forever.

You teach me your language, Maman, but not my sisters. Why? And until some kind soul brews me a drink that will lend me the strength of twelve men, I shall never crack the code, never overthrow the Snow Queen who holds me in her power, forever enthralled.

I am a little girl again, and I hate being so small. I also hate snakes, which are cold and slimy, pulsing back and forth under their devious outer layer of skin. Lester Davidson, who is in my class, makes me hold a garter snake on a dare, and I have nightmares for weeks after. I can never forgive him for the humiliation, but I do not let on to the other kids that he has scared me. *Almighty Father, who seest that we have no power of ourselves to help ourselves; keep us from both outwardly in our bodies and inwardly in our souls; that we may be defended from all adversities which may happen to the body, and from all evil thoughts which may assault and hurt the soul.* Am I dying?

He takes me fishing in the early hours of the morning, the mist still clinging to the lake. I watch in horrified fascination as His penknife slits earthworms in two, the coolness of his quick movements, the smooth wrist action. I know that I too would be capable of such detachment if I ever needed to fish or hunt to survive. I could live outdoors without fear.

When I am bad, I am very bad, and He takes his belt to me, wide and well-worn leather. It hangs on a rusty nail in the basement, and I see it every day on my way to feed the dog.

Maman, I stand before you in my nakedness, skin red and scrubbed from the bath. You try to erase me with a thick Turkish towel. Then we play the game where I am a clown, and you cover my face with spots of white Nivea cream, my spotted mask absurdly cheerful and funny. You wipe off the mask, chanting slowly, Rub it in, rub it in. I think this may be my only memory of us laughing together.

I am watching the film *Bambi*. The scene where Bambi loses his mother makes me want to reach out in the seat beside me, to hold your hand Maman. Trembling all over in fear, warmed by the flames that fill the screen. We leave the cinema by the rear exit, and the sky opens its wrath to us, tears of vengeance, forlorn puddles. Tonight my dreams are of forest fires and melting eyes.

Where are you, Maman? Can you hear me anymore? *A good feminist never blames her mother, understands that all mothers are victims of male oppression. It is misguided to hate your mother, there is enough mother-bashing out there.*
So how will I sing my song, and who will accompany me?

How will I describe the indignities you force me to endure, the way you look away when I need you, the ugly clothing you deliberately choose for me, the cheap food you feed your three daughters while you and He dine on wine and pâté later on? You dress all three of us in identical clothes, three tiny dresses made from one wholesale tablecloth, our garments rent.

You always listen to men, wait for their approval, their judgement. If something disturbs you, you claim it is not your business anyway. How can you understand my horror of being bounced against that hard thing in His lap, the way His tongue just happens to get stuck in my mouth when you tell me to kiss Him goodbye? *That is the way your grandfather shows He loves you.* You listen to everything He says about me; He fills you with venom. Any voice that contradicts is excommunicated, shut out, shielded, no challenges allowed. *Did you hear what I said, young lady? It is your mother you are speaking to, now have some respect.* Perhaps you are the greatest liar of all of us.

I told the man in white that I cannot write anymore, that it is like living twice. I do not want to live. I am dying, after all. I don't want to bother anybody. I must keep breathing. Remember to breathe.

Years of childhood torn asunder, shrouded in secrecy and invisibility. Amnesia as white as the Holy Ghost, as cold as breath in winter.

*Myrrha, Myrrha on the wall, who's the fairest of them all.* You and I are looking in the glass and playing this game, Maman. It is just after my bath. But for you it is never a game. I play it so often that I am convinced my name is Myrrha, that I have a double behind the looking glass. The paradox of Her and Me: to speak with two voices in conflict.

My living is claustrophobic; I occupy only enclosed spaces. I have a secret attic, full of dusty rooms. In my dreams I take my friends on a tour, but only if I really like them. There are several floors, with passageways, hidden staircases, trap doors. One set of stairs leads down into a well-lit room. In the corner there is a revolving door that leads to an adjoining room, a secret escape route, hidden from view. Of all things visible and invisible I hold the key. Occasionally during the tour it becomes necessary for me to leave quickly, before they see the rest, especially the top floor, which is full of cobwebs and very dirty. Old ladies have died up there, their brocade handbags fading into obscurity. I can smell them.

I tell you about this recurring dream, Maman, and you tell me that I have too much imagination, that on our next trip to the public library you will choose the books and there will be no more horror stories or murder mysteries. I do not care, I think I finished all the ones on the shelf anyway, consumed them greedily. But the dream continues, the sequence as familiar as the taste of Friday's fish dinner.

Most of all I remember the stories you read to me about the Snow Country. The fairy tales where little girls are reduced to the size of thumbs and disappear among the wildflowers, lost forever to sight. Where beggar girls die in alleyways on Christmas Eve, burning their last matches, holding out their tiny lights against a darkness that encompasses death but never shrouds grief. I remember the little mermaid who exchanged her tail for one night with her beloved, swallowing the witch's potion and swimming through an underwater channel of weeds, all for that solitary walk across the flagstones on dry land, every step like a knife piercing her feet. *Il faut souffrir pour être belle.* A severed tongue the price to pay for a superior kind of love, the silence of martyrs. And then to be abandoned, deserted, misled. I would lose my tail for you, Maman, endure all pain, except that I know you would not be waiting for me either. The kinship I feel with the little mermaid is real; how can we be bleeding all over the streets with each mincing step forward and no one notice our pain?

I must stop blaming you, Maman. *Stop and smell the roses along the way. Put the past behind you. Live for today.* But what do roses smell like? How will I recognize them when I find them? Trying to forget is the hardest, the flashes of colour come searing through the kitchen window just before dusk, that brief moment when chaos seems resolved in the warm honey glow of late afternoon, drowned by the reassuring clutter of pots and pans. *Enjoy the present, do not dwell on it anymore.* Besides I am probably making this up too. An inventive mind, too many books. *Why are you always living in the past? Why can't you just forgive and forget? It is time to turn a new page in the book of life, turn the other cheek. Just drop it, it is not worth discussing. If you haven't got anything nice to say. . . .*

In my dreams I eat continually but I am never full. So much ice cream and cake. And then I go looking for more. I am caught stealing a frozen pie; I want to be caught, someone to notice what I am doing. No one punishes me though, and I feel disappointed. I want to beg, borrow, or steal what is owed to me, what you cannot give to me: rewards, sweets. Later I fantasize of being strapped in front of the whole school. At first it is just my classmates who watch in awe as the teacher exposes my buttocks while holding me over His knees, but then the other classes file in to watch the spectacle. I shudder with pleasure and shame as the leather belt cracks against my skin. I will not cry even though my face grows as red as a beet. I have this fantasy repeatedly; it is like watching a rerun of a favourite movie. I wake up in a puddle of urine, the smell comforting in its familiarity. *This is a normal fantasy; it is natural for girls to be masochistic.*

We still live in the old country, the Snow Land. It is the same ritual every night, the one you devised so long ago, Maman. You first kiss me on both cheeks, a cold and icy formality because you never let me see what your eyes are saying as you turn your face to either side, as if in disgust or embarrassment. You tell me you love me. I am expected to respond dutifully, I love you too, Maman. Then you turn away.

*Sleep well. See you in the morning.*

Sinyras is His name. The one who comes to my bed at night. They all say I asked for it. *You made me do it, you little whore.* I cannot pronounce His name out loud, but I know it sounds like Sinner. A small sin. Just a little white lie.

I wrote a letter to Maman, and on the way I dropped it.
A little doctor picked it up and put it in His pocket
And He won't bite me, and He won't bite you
But He'll bite the one who's got it.

So drop it, so drop it,
We'll all look behind.

I am seven years old.  I am learning a new language.  The teacher comes from Cambridge; she is young and pretty and I admire her clothes.  I imitate her accent walking home from school, the singing cadence of her voice.  She praises my quickness.  There are many other countries where I can use my English.  My cousin has been to Canada to visit an aunt and uncle.  She says that in Canada you can be whatever you want to be.  I decide that day that no one will stop me from going there.  I tell the teacher my plan to move to London, Ontario, to live with my aunt and uncle.  She says that I am mistaken, that there is only one London, and it is in England, where she comes from.  For a long time I think of it as my imaginary city.  It does not matter to me if it is real or not.  Just learning another language makes the pain go away; the words are not the same.

*We will play animals now.  I am going to be the dog.  You have to go and hide and I will sniff you out.  Ha, Ha!  I found you.  Now kiss the puppy's nose.  Here, lick it.  It's wet, just like your dog Tutti's nose, isn't it?  See, He likes it.  Don't worry, He won't bite you.*

He laughs at me for wearing glasses, calls me brainy.  The glasses are cat's eyes, old-fashioned, all He can afford, baby blue with silver sparkles.  I hate wearing them, have guilty wishes of dropping them down the sewer grating.  I hatch plots for destroying them, but none is perfect.  I would still be blamed.  He hits me every time I do not wear them, says that in a few years I will have coke bottle lenses if I do not smarten up.  *You are asking for it.*  In my dreams, the glasses fly through space, shattering on contact with the wall like ceramic plates.  I cannot stop the pieces from falling everywhere;  against my skin they feel like the soft sting of raindrops.  Everything I touch becomes broken, tainted with ugliness.

*I did not mean to do it.* I stole the wart ointment from the corner pharmacy, thinking that I had a wart on my arm. The scab had not gone away for weeks, and I picked it over and over again. I keep it covered with a Bandaid, apply the wart-removing acid every day. Soon I can see only whitish bubbles under the Bandaid, and the hole is getting larger. I am fascinated, cannot stop. There are so many scars on my body I cannot explain. But this one I remember vividly.

Maman, you convince me that the glass liner for my thermos bottle is precious; I believe it must be very expensive, since you explode when I announce my thermos has broken when I put my schoolbag down on the sidewalk. After that, when I bring home my empty thermos bottle from school in my school bag, I am terrified of dropping it, of hearing the inevitable tinkling sound. I never understand why I cannot buy a cardboard carton of milk at school like my classmates do, why I cannot be the same as everyone else.

I cannot make mistakes. *Mistakes are not allowed.* She will suffer if I make too many mistakes. My soul is getting pitch black. First comes purgatory, then hell.

*Now I lay me down to sleep. I pray the Lord my soul to keep. And if I die before I wake, I pray the Lord my soul to take.* But my soul is no good; take my body instead; I don't care about my body, it is ugly and dirty. Just keep my soul in heaven and I will fly away and never have to come back down here again.

I always live close to that razor-sharp edge. I read *The Diary of Anne Frank* and realize that she must be my true sister, that only she knows what it feels like to be hunted every day, to hide from the Nazis. I read the passage where she describes the rotating wall carefully concealed behind the bookcase in a room. Then I refer to the secondhand encyclopedia set you picked up at a church sale, and glance at the chapter on building techniques at the back. There are blueprints for bookshelves, tree forts, but nothing practical like hideaways or secret doorways. Disappointment gnaws at my stomach like unassuaged hunger.

Maman, I wish you could be here to confirm my pictures from the past, the memories of which I can only be vaguely certain, fill in the details in your anecdotal manner, your eye for detail. The way you remember what Aunt Marie was wearing on her fortieth birthday, the colour of the tablecloth at the restaurant, what everyone ordered and how it tasted. How much of a tip was left for the waitress. And His contempt, the way He shuns your talent. *Frivolous details.*

Now the whole family is moving to Canada. We live with my aunt and uncle until the new house is built. I study the frame of the new house in Northridge, its skeletal beginnings, the thicket of mosquitoes in the bush waiting to attack me as the two of you look over the construction site. When it is finished, I see that this is a sinister house: its face is painted white, the black shutters are fringed eyelashes that watch me enter and exit, and stare haughtily after me. The door is an open gaping mouth, a wide gash waiting to swallow me up as soon as I put my foot on the doorstep. If I close my eyes, I can will the house to spiral away into the air, whirling upwards in a blur. The memory tastes salty; the slap of mosquitoes on my forearm, blood running unnoticed down my legs. He wants to show me the woods that will be my new playground; only eight weeks until we move in.

I borrow the same library book every Saturday. It is *The Lonely Doll* by Dare Wright. It is full of real black and white photographs, and Edith gets to wear lots of beautiful, short dresses, with pretty crinolines sticking out underneath. Edith has everything a little girl could want except friends. Even the pigeons want nothing to do with her, and there is no one to talk to at breakfast. She is like me: people turn away from her instinctively, as if she were contaminated. Every night she prays for a playmate. When Mr. Bear meets her, He pats her on the head and assures her that He and Little Bear will be her friends. They take her to the beach, and on fishing trips. But He scolds her when she gets dirty or does anything without His permission. Her pretty underclothes always show when He takes her over His knees to spank her. When Edith is alone with Little Bear, they play in her mother's closet, and she dresses up in petticoats and high heels, and stares at herself in the mirror. *My hair looks dreadful, and I'm tired of this old dress.* Little Bear tells her that all she needs is lipstick. *Oh, I'd never dare. Mr. Bear would not let me do that. Who cares what Mr. Bear says, I don't,* says Little Bear. He grabs the lipstick and scribbles *Mr. Bear is a silly old thing* across the mirror, but Edith can see Mr. Bear in the mirror as He approaches from behind. *You are too young for lipstick.* A courageous and defiant voice emerges from nowhere: *I am not. And I don't care what you say anyway, you're just a silly.* Mr. Bear is very angry now. *I may be a silly, but I know when a naughty little girl needs a spanking.* Little Bear complains that girls just cry when they get spanked. I know that this is not true: I am often spanked and I never cry. *It is not that,* says Edith, *I'm scared because Mr. Bear is so angry. What if He goes away and takes you with Him?* After they tidy the room, Edith and Little Bear find Mr. Bear in his black leather recliner, reading the newspaper. Edith apologizes profusely, and Mr. Bear forgives her. *Perhaps we can forget all about it, put it behind us. Promise you will stay with me forever?*

Maman, I remember the little sparrow I found in the alleyway with the broken wing. How gingerly I carry it home in an old detergent carton. Carefully you and I feed it sunflower seeds and water from an eye dropper. I ask if it will die, and you say never, *nothing ever really dies,* we will put it in a cardboard box and put it up high on top of the refrigerator where it is nice and warm. I rush home from school to check its progress the next day, and look on top of the refrigerator, but the box is not there. I find you in the basement, and ask you what has happened to our bird. *Gone to heaven, the mother came along and mended its broken wing. The last time I saw the pair they were soaring upwards together, singing happily.* It is not until the trash goes out at the end of the week that I find it, the box bent in two, the carcass stiff and grey, crumpled and stuck to one of the sides of its cardboard bed.

51

I am a clumsy girl, always breaking bones, never at one with my body. My body seems to have a will all its own, falling over things; I have no control over its movements, except a delayed reaction to the pain of it having made a mistake, misjudged the curb height. I can only react, never act.

Like Edith, I break into your closet, try on your clothes. Apply lipstick and test the mirror for its effects. Look, I am in your shoes now. Will you still love me when you find out how rotten I am inside?

On your bureau dresser is a little china figurine of a bird that you brought with you from that other country, so delicate that I am afraid to dust it, lest I break it. *Clumsy girl.*

He is playing a game with me. He says that we should pretend we are logs and lie like this, arms tucked behind our backs, at the top of the hill, and roll down together. The newly-mown grass smells of summer; it is sweet and warm. Springbank Park, near the Children's Garden. We roll and roll until I feel dizzy, and I laugh hysterically. Suddenly I feel His weight on top of me. I cannot move. I think I have struck a tree at the bottom of the hill, the one that spun around me in my whirlwind glimpses of the sky and the ground as I was rolling down. Maybe I am dead, trapped in a kaleidoscope that will not stop turning. I cannot breathe. Above me the heavens spin round and round, white pillow clouds stretched by thin cotton strands at their borders. Light of light, the eternally blue and white sky gapes above me; begotten; not made of candy floss after all.

I have no pictures of you, Maman, of our time together. Only a black and white picture of you on your confirmation day, your conversion to His religion two weeks before your marriage. You seem so young, so unsure of yourself. I wish my memories had colours. Like Red, who is angry all the time and keeps interrupting me when I try to be good. I no longer know who I am. She writes differently in this book, her letters are large and scrawl across the page, as if she comes into my room at night and writes when I am asleep.

Green is full of bile. She chokes and sputters when people pay her compliments, and she is constantly getting sick. Red despises her for being so weak. The Blue Lady says to forgive her, She says to forgive you too, but I do not know anymore. The Blue Lady is so ethereal. She came to visit me for the first time in grade one. She is just a piece of blue chiffon that floats in front of me like a ballet dancer. At first Her voice is barely audible. The truth is that I do not want to hear Her. Then I realize that She speaks another language, soft cooing French consonants. She is nothing like me. She radiates blue tranquility, waves of tenderness that sometimes nauseate me with their sweetness. Her intensity and idealism sicken me. She is naive and innocent, open and vulnerable. But Her voice continues to haunt me. I even see her when I am awake; She is a soft blue light joined to me at my solar plexus, looking straight into my eyes. She looks like Glinda the Good Witch from *The Wizard of Oz*. She will grant me my every wish, but asks me to consider carefully before I ask. She is always there when I need her. *Ding dong, the witch is dead, the wicked witch is dead.* Take me away with you, Glinda, with a wave of your wand make all of this pass.

Why are these women so colourful, when my memories are only black or white? Do they come from me? I think I might be making them up. But they are my only friends, even if they are imaginary, and they live inside me all the time. I want to let all these colours open wide and speak to you, Maman. Release them from the black and white cage of the heart.

No, it is not true. I have one beautiful picture of you in my memory. We are sitting in a field of spring flowers, just outside the new subdivision development. I watch your magic fingers weaving a crown of daisies. When it is finished, you place it ceremoniously on my head. The stems hurt my scalp and stick into my ears. I do not mind that it hurts because I remember your message that it takes great pain to be beautiful, and I want to be beautiful like you are. You tell me I am a flower princess. The sun is very hot on my back and you are smiling.

He returns from a business trip, bearing gifts for all. Maman, you were not allowed to go with Him, so you stayed home, paced the floors, smoked. I want to dance with you when you put the radio on after supper, sleep in your bed. *No, you are a big girl now.*

The voices have always mocked me. They tell me I cannot do anything right, I am a failure. Some days I manage to tune them out. At other times they overwhelm me and I feel crippled; I lie in bed unable to move. When they tell me to hurt myself, I obey instinctively. They tell me to lie so that no one will find out. To separate the personal from the public or I will never survive. The voice of the Editor, harsh in her criticism, says that I should rip all these pages up, show them to no one, especially the man in white. She hisses at me—*He is like all the others.* The Editor looks for spelling errors, says I do not have my facts straight, that all of this is hearsay. She slips into a hospital dressing gown and slippers in the middle of the night, glides across the floor, and destroys all the pages I write by day. I am afraid of her; she is my Persecutor. And then there is another voice that tells me that I must speak to you. I must listen to Her, stop being afraid of what She says. She tells me that my inner demon is harsher on me than I am. If I can stop being afraid of the Editor, external critics, the ones living outside my head will never harm me again. I think She may be right.

Your rage is palpable. *Don't ever take candy from a stranger.* Slowly I unfurl the foil-wrapped evidence in my sweaty palm and hand it over to you. With my head bowed in shame, I march back to the end of the street to tell the man who is tending his garden that my mother says no.

It is cold in church. The holy water from the font, which I dabbed on my neck in imitation of you applying perfume, has dried on my skin. The wooden benches are sticky from other palms, the naugahide is depressed under my knees from the last person who knelt in prayer. You are annoyed that we missed the early mass, Maman, because there is so much work to do when you get home. Our parish priest is coming for dinner, and you are thinking about what needs thawing. The sermon drones on and on. Only scattered words reach me. *Sew as ye shall rape. My brethren, we must join in our support for the souls of* . . . A white hot pain fills my belly. I grip my rosary harder, and the church is filled with coloured light. A cloud has lifted outside, and the sun cascades through stained glass. Stained the colour of blood, the colour of night, the stations of the cross soldered in lead. A mosaic of suffering; purple cloth draped everywhere; the taste of guilt at the pit of my stomach. Or maybe just hunger. *Give us this day our daily.*

He is unobtrusive-looking. He reads the second reading every Sunday. A lay reader. He wears the new suit you had made for Him, Maman, to celebrate His promotion with the company. In church the words are slow and full of emphasis, every one is a hidden message for me, He is warning me that He knows what I am thinking. At home He speaks in French when He is angry, the words thick and venomous. *How will I ever succeed in business with the damned anglais and their tightass control of the market. The Jews and the English, they are no good. My English must get better. When Mémé and Pépé come to visit next time, there will be no French under my roof, do you hear? It is all assbackwards, their patois. Stupid peasoupistes, mes parentes. And here I thought I had moved away from all that, goddammit. In our house we speak English only.*

*Of course I love you, what a silly question. And Daddy does too.* He says He loves me, that I can depend on Him. He is the boss in the family, His word goes. I want Him to love me. *I only have your health and welfare in mind. Daddy knows what is best for you. This hurts me more than it hurts you. I am doing it for your own good, because I love you.*

I stare and stare at the television set. He is snoring loudly, and He forgot to tell me He loved me, even after it is all over. Kennedy has been assassinated, the television blares in the background, the pictures flicker in black and white and then my mind goes blank, *do not adjust your set. We do not know who the Enemy is.* I memorize the cracks on the black naugahide couch, the smells of sweat and scalp, and then trace the dark patches where flesh ripping against sticky blackness leaves a temporary wet mark, evaporating like Windex on the surface of the stove. *The inner core of American life has been destroyed, our national sense of justice and decency will never be the same.* The decade passes me by where I lie on the couch, the images condensed. I am floating again. *A giant step for mankind.* Weightless, my head trapped in a bubble somewhere, where troubles melt like lemondrops.

In the mornings, you straighten the cushions on the couch. *I ordered double cheese. They must have got it wrong again.* Throw out the newspaper. Glaring headlines hold no interest for you. You want Him to read it as quickly as possible so you can gather all the papers up and throw them in the fireplace. *Everything in its place, and a place for everything.* The only thing you had no place for was me. Iphigenia as disposable as the stale crusts of pizza and the cardboard box you toss to the flames. *Did they put enough pepperoni on this time?*

The holes on the surface of the moon grow larger, our first close-ups.  Not made of cheese after all.  The dark crevices unexplored, gaping holes. *Mare crisum.*

We are going through the House of Mirrors, there are so many versions of my mother and me, endless replications, first thin, then fat, my sisters are caught in the room behind but I can hear their voices.  Then it is just me alone, I have lost my mother and there is only my distorted and bloated face ahead of me, threads of candy floss glued to my fingers.

The devastation continues.  The holes on the surface of my skin, scabs from mosquito bites, grow larger and larger.  I should stop picking at them.

After I finish my chores, I bury myself in detective novels, dream of finding the perfect plan, murder without a hitch, no traces.

All I remember is absence, your coldness and indifference. *Daddy is under a lot of pressure right now. He needs a drink.* Thinking it is my fault that He drinks all the time. I make Him do that.

w  h  i  t  e    l  i  e  s    (  f  o  r    m  y    m  o  t  h  e  r  )

Maman, do you remember bringing home the green plastic winter coat from that cheap department store, with the plush lining? Snot green, the kids call it. It is ugly, three sizes too large. *How can you be so ungrateful, when there are children in this world who have nothing at all to wear? It is all we can afford. How would you like to be naked in the middle of winter?* Your nails thrust into my shoulders to reinforce the point. Ice pink, frosted I think, by Revlon. And the crumpled bag on the floor with your new, expensive gold lamé evening dress. You never liked me; wanted to sting me with your words, would rather I was dead. *What will I do with you,* you wring your hands over and over again.

*Why didn't you resist?* I was afraid to say no, afraid He might hurt you even more. You never tell me about my body, except to say that I am too plump. I thought it was because He loved me, that all fathers showed their affection that way, did not know what this was called. The only time the possibility existed of His being gentle with me, of paying attention to me at all. When what I really wanted was your attention, Maman.

In the mornings, you come to wake me, pull back the curtains and let the sun in. I ache all over, Maman, I can't get out of bed. The pain sears through my body like fire, I feel as though I have bruises on every inch of my skin. But nothing shows at all. *You are acting like the princess who pretends she cannot sleep because there is a pea under her seventeen mattresses. Now don't be silly.*

I have memorized every crack in the linoleum, every chipped tile, all of the water stains on the stucco ceiling in the bathroom at my grandparents' house. I can describe in full detail the crocheted costume of the doll whose skirt conceals the spare toilet paper roll; she sits on the back of the toilet, and I know every skipped stitch, every colour transition in the wool, the blue of her cheaply-painted, bleary eyes. I lock myself in the bathroom for hours. I hear someone pounding on the door, but I refuse to come out. I run my fingers over the cool porcelain of the bathtub. Red tells me to ignore the knocking and pretend I am the toilet paper doll.

School is cancelled. The rage of Demeter knows no bounds; the snow is piled in our stairwell and we cannot even open the door to go out and play. I read the same book over and over. You stay in the other room. We avoid looking at each other, do not know what to say to each other. Where was your anger then, why did you never want to rescue me from my frozen state? The snow punishment lasts seven days, and then the doors of the schoolyard's linked fence open once again like eager arms to embrace us back to our fractions.

Your hands, again, come to haunt me. If passion exists in this world, surely it rests in those hands and what they can teach me, hands now idly crossed on your lap as I sit once more beside you in church. How much I want them to hold me. *Only hold my hand, and I shall be healed.*

*Come out, come out wherever you are.* Little girl, I know you are hiding. You have all the pieces to the puzzle, the pictures that get first prize, the perfect handwriting that gets the gold star. Not this uneven script. That belongs to Red. I write small, then big, slanted left or big, fat, up-and-down letters when I feel strong. Mostly they are skinny and slant to the right. Do you notice that when you steal my diary, Maman? I know that you have come into the room to see what I have written. Big and fat and strong letters, up and down like a yoyo. This tremulous cry, epistolary wail, chicken scratch I have saved for you all these years, waiting to be unravelled. Everything gets swept under the bed here, even crumpled pieces of paper. Nobody ever looks there. Maybe they are important to me, maybe I want to keep them. But there is company coming. *We need to clear this all up now.*

*Liar liar your pants are on fire. Hang them on the telephone wire.* You are picking up all our clothes to do the laundry. My cotton underpants lie crumpled and soaked under the bed, my flannel pyjama bottoms beside them. Your sigh is heavy as you bend over to reach for them. Sorting into categories, cold and hot. Black and white. Already ahead of yourself, thinking of items to add to your grocery list, you see nothing. You change my sheets every Saturday, Maman. Don't you smell anything funny, notice the stains, the wet spots? *A late bedwetter.*

In the beginning, I want to save you, to take you away, to build you a castle in the land where you came from, to buy you a horse. I dream you hoist me up in your saddle. He said that what I do is helping you, that you always do it for Him, but that I should now that you are sick. And so for a long time I believe I am you. He says I look just like you, His weight on me as heavy as guilt.

It makes me happy when He says I look like you. I think you are beautiful. I love to hold your hand in church, twisting the diamonds around on your finger, watching the light play on those brilliant stones, marvelling at the long blue rivers that wind themselves around your wrist and snake their way up to the top of your hands. I run my rough fingertips, the nails bit ragged, along the edges of your perfectly-filed nails, wrap my stubby fingers around your elegance. Suddenly you notice me, stop staring distractedly at the altar, slap my hand. But for those brief moments when your hand accidentally squeezes mine, I feel dizzy with happiness, all the colours of the world stream through these stained glass windows, sing anthems of praise to your hands.

On the drive back from church, you turn to face me, *What has gotten into you, why don't you pay attention anymore? I don't know what has happened to this one.* Later in the afternoon light, your face grows wistful, staring at an old photo album, turning the pages slowly with those immaculate hands. *You were such an angel as a baby.* His voice snarls from the other side of the room, *Yeah, what happened to you now?* And your face freezes as his laughter peels away the air.

So little to remember about you.  I wish I knew more.  I am tempted to invent you, attach the floating bodies of my dreams to your face.  Occasionally something that matches comes to me, but then I waken too quickly, disappointed.  Fleeting like a ghost, a woman who might have been there, might not.

This is my dilemma:  You simply are not there.  A phantom besieged by miscarriages and nervous breakdowns.  I recall only your absences.  Your appearance of strength:  *Bébert, pas devant les enfants. We never argue.*  The cushions get fluffed and there is never any silence or dangerous pause in which to reflect; words mask panic; we are constantly busy with family activities.

I try to fill your shoes, to make the breadcrumb coating for the meat in the medium-sized Tupperware bowl as you would, stack the bowls neatly, fitting one into the other before putting them away in the cupboard. Every time I cook liver I shudder at the contact with that cold raw limp flesh, gelatinous and vulnerable.

I am eight years old. He rages at me that I am a hopeless case. I train my sisters to dry the dishes and stack them properly, to wipe the stove and countertop, remove sticky fingerprints from all the appliances. If I do it just right, He will not punish me this time. If I could just get it right once. Green tells me I am useless. If I could only be perfect. Remember to sweep all the crumbs from under the table, mix the powdered milk to be ready for breakfast, make my sisters' lunches. Plan the next meal, leftovers, see what needs to be put on the grocery list. Wipe the counter. Turn out the stove light.

The body remembers first. Not my own body; I can feel nothing. But the memories sear through the skin like fire, and I have no control over the sensations. The odour of mustard as He makes a poultice for my chest, rubbing it too vigorously, patting down the undershirt on top. The heat plunges beneath the skin and I am terrified. This is an old family remedy for colds, He says. *As my father did unto me, so shall I do unto you.*

*The night cometh when no man can work.* He is always there. Waiting for me. Or else, saying I am going to bed early to read, I lie in bed and watch the light fill the crack under the door, listen for the heavy creak of footsteps on the floorboards, moaning under worn carpet, wait to hear the bathroom door close, listen for the snap that ends the buzz of the fluorescent light, my heart thumping wildly. Each sound familiar, anguished. Finally the door closes, echoing hollowness. The glow-in-the-dark crucifix takes over the darkness; each quiver of the bedsprings becomes a line from the Hail Mary, or a verse from a song on the hit parade. The hot wet mouth is the Holy Spirit's gift of fire; I speak in tongues, a spitball of unknown powers, intelligible only to God. That I am His chosen, the special one, is the only thing I know. Our family secret, a promise not to tell Maman or my sisters, who could get jealous. I think of the Family Compact in my history class, I think of God, and the Holy Spirit who connects Him to His son, the most special family of all.  Most of all I pray:  that the burning pain inside will stop soon, that the cold wetness will signal the end for now.  That this will make you get better, Maman.  The necessity of sacrifice.  Maybe a miracle; I could be just like all the saints I admire.  Maybe your babies will stop dying in your belly, Maman.  Maybe I won't get on your nerves so much. *Love suffers long, love is kind, enduring all things, hoping all things.*

I dream of becoming a nun. I see a film called *The Trouble with Angels* and a chord is struck deep within me. Hayley Mills is just like me; she has Red's anger and also has strong spiritual yearnings. In the final scene it is clear that one girl must stay behind. It is me. I am chosen. A voice calling. *The mystery of the veil,* Sister Mary Marthe calls it. The voice of the Blue Lady.

One night I stay over at my friend's house, and she tells me how babies are made. A man puts his stick in a woman's pee-pee hole, and a baby comes out. I tell her this is a lie, and I grow red in the face. I am not sure why it is a lie, but somehow I know that it is different. She says I do not know anything. I am two years younger than she is, after all. A week later, I lie on a grassy hill, thinking about what she said; the black hole festering inside me might really be a baby. Maybe I could have a baby and then you would not have to go to the hospital so much, Maman. You always look so tired. *To give is more blessed than to receive.* I would like to give you a baby. I ask my friend how the baby is supposed to come out, and she says they cut a hole in your stomach with a knife. *Whose God is their belly, and whose glory is their shame.*

It is the same memory that haunts me, the salty waves of hot words trapped inside my throat, the broken jaw that He insists I got falling out of my wagon. The way I get up to speak in public and feel choked, sick, the nauseous sentences caught in my throat, the bile rising from the dark hole inside. Hand clutching at my throat each night. Even years later, its phantom grip overpowers me. But I will speak, Maman. I must speak. I can no longer save you. I am not sure I can even love you anymore. My mouth is so full that no words can come out, even those in your language from the old country, our language. *What has passed our lips as food, may we possess in purity of heart, that what is given to us in time, be our healing for eternity.*

*Shut up and do what I say. If you cannot close your mouth then I guess I will have to do it for you. Open up wide. Thatta girl.*

*And on the third day He rose again,* and makes me clean up all the empty beer bottles before you come home. I like putting your house back in order, Maman. Just the way you expect it to look. I tell my sisters not to disturb Him as long as He sleeps on the couch. We are instructed to tell anyone who calls that He is out of town, He says, *a small white lie because Daddy is not feeling well.*

Maman, you teach me to roll out the dough. Again I am admiring your deft hands. You stand with the pie pin in your hands above me, a magic wand that will miraculously transform the work of my sticky little fingers into flaky crust for the Christmas tortière. I am kneeling on a chair to reach the kitchen table, its surface floured. The dough is soft, malleable, like my baby sister's skin. I feel happy to help you. Suddenly you are angry. *You are always ruining everything.* My hot little hands have killed the dough. I turn the pie pin over and over on the table so I won't cry, I roll away all the bad thoughts, squish them out into something smooth and seamless.

Maman, you always say you are too fat. You stand in front of the mirror and pinch the folds of skin over your stomach and your face fills with despair. Or you twist your face when you cook in the kitchen, a horrible grimace. *Could you help me open this jar?* That tiny laugh of yours. *I am really quite stupid, don't know what I would do without Him. He is my rock, my pillar of strength.* Your body bent in humility, or sitting with one leg twisted around the other under the kitchen chair like a vine around an arbor, your hands nervously fluttering around your face or clutching a cigarette. The only time you stand tall and straight is by the side of a horse, a different woman for one moment, a strong commanding tone of voice—*you must let the horse know who is boss*—a lady in tall, shiny leather boots and a fuzzy brown hat. You are confident, serene. You tell me stories about wanting a horse more than anything in the world, how you gave it up to get married and move to this country. There are medals and dusty ribbons in the attic in our house, which only you are allowed to dust. The photograph I love best is sepia-toned: a young woman with a healthy glow running her fingers through the horse's mane. I am so proud of you in this picture.

I moan, I cry, and I rock myself from side to side, but it hurts too much. There is a story I read about a girl who has the stigmata of Christ, who wakes up with holes in her hands and her side, the blood streaming forth. In the picture in the story, her face is beatific, she wears a yellow halo, and people come from all around to see her. Maybe this is what is happening to me, I am being tested to see if I am good enough to become a saint. Maybe if I am good and patient enough, everyone will worship me for my holiness, believe I am special. Like the Virgin Mary, I want to keep my soul as pure as Hers so that I too will be lifted up to heaven and be spared the indignity of rotting in a dark moldy grave.

I am cruel to my little sister. I hate her innocent little face, how easily her big, dopey eyes fill with tears. It is so easy to hit her over and over again, because when it is over I can always kiss her, tell her I am sorry, and she will forgive me. That is the sweetest part. She is so stupid and defenceless. I tell her I am going to be nice to her today instead; we'll play a game called frogs which I invent on the spot. I make her lie down on the floor and I straddle her, jumping up and down. Don't you think leap frog means you jump over top of me? she asks. No, this is my game. I like hurting her. I only stop riding her when I have had enough. *Stop, you are hurting me.*

*Stop crying. Silly girl. It is only a game.*

In grade five, I am selected to attend a special school located downtown. I take the city bus to get there. Advanced class, for smart kids. Now I am certain I am special. While waiting for the bus, which comes only once an hour, I steal candy from the corner store to impress the other kids. It is easy; I think they are beginning to like me. At the end of the year, the teacher asks me to stay after school one day. She holds a library book in her hands that I recognize; it is a large volume about horses with many coloured pictures. She removes the borrower's card from the back and points out that I have signed the book out more than twenty times this year. I acknowledge that this is true, I tell her I love horses. Inside the dust jacket, under the plastic flap, there is a crude drawing of male genitals and what appears to be a bird's nest; in the margins there is a pencil sketch of two horses fused together; beneath it, a vulgar description of the sex act in graphic terms. I blush fiercely, tell her I have never seen this before. Is this a white lie or a black lie? *It wasn't me.* The librarian walks down the hallway, retrieves the book and glances knowingly at my teacher. My teacher tells me that we have discussed Reproduction in class, that there is no need to write about it in this coarse manner. I need to see a special counsellor. She will speak to my family and arrange a time. I feel dread all day, the pit in my stomach expanding with each passing hour. Next week my parents are told that I will not be allowed to return to this school because I am not emotionally mature. You repeat this to me, but I do not understand what it means.

We are at the family counsellor's office. He is a man with a grey beard. My sisters giggle, and you fidget with your purse catch, avoiding the accusatory stare of your husband. His voice is louder than usual. He is angry, he points at me. *Here is the problem. We have done everything possible. Maybe you can tell us what to do with her.* His eyes dart wildly about the room. He cannot sit still in his chair, but His agitation is noticed only by me. Tonight it will be bad, I can tell. I am quiet, I say nothing. *Uncooperative. Sometimes they're just born rebellious.* He is telling lies.

We have to attend more sessions. Once, upon returning from a family psychotherapy session, He stops at a drugstore and buys me a poster of a cat dangling from a pole which reads, "Hang in there, baby." He gives me the usual lecture about how I need to turn over a new leaf. The cat looks terrified, its eyes bulging.

We are allowed to watch television only on weekend nights. Do you remember, Maman? *Too much T.V. is bad for children.* The forbidden fruit. One Saturday afternoon I am alone with my sisters, and I turn the black and white set on, in spite of their protests. *It will only be a white lie if we do not tell Maman.* We watch an old Dracula movie. I am fascinated by the scene where the vampire is killed, the stake pounded into His heart, blood spurting. My sisters scream, but I cannot unglue my eyes. My heart pounds rapidly. I learn that if I keep a crucifix over my bed at night, the vampires will be scared away. Hanging garlic over me will have the same effect. I steal garlic from the basement and put it under my bed, so that you will not discover it, Maman. I have nightmares for weeks after. Some nights after He leaves, I know all of my blood has been drained and I only have a little life left. I take the crucifix off the wall and clutch it to my heart. From then on I vow to sleep with the blankets twisted around my neck, to avoid exposing my vulnerable throat to a thirsty vampire.

In grade six, She makes me start smoking in the girls' bathroom at school, hiding myself in the stall, locking the door. The cigarettes taste terrible, fill my lungs with a delicious and heavy pressure. Red only wants me to get caught; She does not really enjoy this. When no one comes to stop me, She makes me set a match to the paper towels in the wastepaper container. The flames leap out from the white metal cylinder, graying the edges. Divine sacrifice. She feels excited by the flames, mesmerized by the rapidity with which they spread. *We don't stop for nobody, we don't stop for nobody*, Red sings defiantly. Her voice comes from nowhere. The teacher questions all the girls later, and She makes me tell a white lie to protect Her. We do not want to get punished again. *You are always trying to attract attention. You have to be different, don't you. Well, young lady we will see who is boss here.* Others admire Her daring, the way She talks back to the teachers. It is Red you are talking to now, Maman.

We are going to visit some family friends named the Wilsons. Mr. Wilson is also a pilot in the air force. Just like Him. While you the adults are all smoking and drinking around the kitchen table, She makes me carve my initials and the S.O.S. into their new oak dining room table. No one notices me. Mr. Wilson calls next week, you march me back to the house to apologize. *But it was not me who did it, it was Her, this is no lie.* On the way out, Mr. Wilson sits behind his newspaper as if nothing has happened, I have to make the apology to his wife, furniture is not his business. He looks like the polar bear who chases me in my dreams; his brown eyes have a glassy yellow glint in the centre, almost as if he were winking at me. He has gold-capped front teeth that catch the light.

For His birthday I go to the department store with my babysitting money in my red plastic purse. I buy monogrammed handkerchiefs with the letter A stitched in bright blue. By contrast the linen looks too white, as if you would never want to use it to blow your nose or to wipe up anything dirty.

My grade seven gym teacher takes me aside in the teachers' room. I realize that I have never seen her smoke before; she looks like a different person. She wonders why I always become hysterical when she chooses sides for the volleyball team; if I am not chosen immediately, I sit huddled in the corner of the gym and cry until she comes over to console me. I accuse her of not loving me.

He has orchestrated it perfectly. He attends all the P.T.A. meetings, even if it means taking time off work. He never lets you go alone, Maman, never allows you to leave His side. *How romantic, he cares about me so much.* He approaches my teacher carefully in the discussion period following the meeting and seeks her professional advice about what to do with a child who has behavioural problems. *My wife and I have tried everything.*

I have a friend who is exactly the same age as I am. She too wants to be a nun. After we have been friends all year, played on the volleyball team together, I ask her if she will come to stay overnight at my house in the springtime. She does, but she is clearly uncomfortable around my father, tells me He has bulging eyes and wandering hands. Years later tells me that she was so terrified of Him that she refused to ever sleep overnight at my house again, despite my pleas.

My first period begins.  One of the sisters tells us that this means the womb is weeping because conception has not occurred.  I want to be like the Virgin Mary.  I think I may be bleeding to death.  He has really done it this time.  I am not certain what is happening to me.

The notebook is fuller, but He has not asked to look at it yet. Should I continue?

w h i t e    l i e s    ( f o r    m y    m o t h e r )

I may not come out alive, but I'm going in there.

I pick up my daughter at the daycare and nurse her in a room adjoined to the nursery. The janitor enters the room at the precise moment when I lift my shirt. He stares long and hard. I feel exposed, invaded. He takes his time sweeping and then mopping the floor. The next day I change rooms, but he arrives there too, his big toothy grin and a "hi, sweetheart" for my baby. Such a sweet old man, harmless, worldweary expression, dragging his feet. The oppressed working class, subject to harassment from students. My grandfather is also a janitor, but is usually called peasouper, pig, dirty old trash man, cleaning up other peoples' messes. Why does this one bother me so much, what memory does he trigger? Why do I go home depressed and shaking?

Discord. There is something strange about the music that circles in my head all day, but I cannot make it go away, my ears are ringing. Then just as suddenly it stops. The dentist has me tilted back in his chair. My mouth is stuffed with wads of cotton batting, and my jaw is clamped in place by two metal prongs. *Just a fluoride treatment.* But I feel like I am going to gag, I want to scream. My daughter cries in the waiting room, the nurse's voice trying to calm her, muted female voices from another world. I close my eyes and everything turns black, melts into the recognizable realm of safety. *How long since your last check-up?* I am a little girl again in the confessional, and the voice of the priest reaches out for me in the darkness. *How long since your last confession?* The voice of authority; the instruments of power; the ability to forgive, the cold taste of metal that fixes everything. I have just told my parish priest what He does to me at home. I am afraid, since the priest often comes to our house for dinner. He tells me I should try to understand that Father is under a great deal of pressure, that my mother is very sick, and that He is having a hard time managing without her right now.

It is midnight mass on Christmas Eve, and my grandfather sings *O Holy Night, the stars are brightly shining, fall on your knees.* He is known all over the parish for his singing. The whole church is full of praise for his deep tenor voice; we sing this song again at his funeral and everyone else is in tears but me. I do not understand that people can cry about something beautiful, or from sheer astonishment that this triumphant voice can emerge from such a twisted form. One of my aunts grips the pew so tightly that her knuckles turn white.

I read about Greek mythology in a large picture book from the library. The picture I like best is of Daphne running away, turning into a beautiful tree, sprouting green leaves. How marvellous it would be to be able to hide yourself that way. I think of growing leaves from my bitten fingernails, of sprouting roots and watching them sink into the ground. Not as punishment from Zeus. But as camouflage, protection. After reading this story, I walk in the woods and regard the trees with new respect.

Maman, rescue me from all these crazy gods. I will care for you when you get old and grey, continue your work for you. How can you let Him take me away? Yet how can you save me either, you who were also twice-born, twice raped, your strength and thunder stolen by Zeus and then Poseidon when you crossed the sea to come to this country, a small baby wrapped in your arms? In me you live on.

Adam disobeyed his Father. But if I were Eve, where would I find my mother? The juice spurts everywhere, delicious, forbidden fruit, the taste of guilt and pleasure inextricably blended. *What you are doing is holding the family together. I am proud of you for keeping our secret, for doing what I tell you. And your mother would be too. But it is better not to look for praise, to keep it our secret.*

The pictures come faster:  His absurdly erect nipples with two hairs attached to one pectoral muscle, the only upper body hair, except for under His armpits, I never look lower than that.  His alligator skin, rounded shoulders, the smell of stale wine on His breath, the cold clammy feel of sweat drying on His skin.  Flashbacks are triggered by smell, by touch.  The terror is palpable; the reasons, never clear.  *Hail Mary, full of grace, the Lord is with Thee.*

My only gift from Him:  a watch for my confirmation, a very expensive one.  I enjoy the look of disbelief on the clerk's face at the counter in the Sally Ann, when I hand it to her and tell her to give it to someone who needs it.  My act of rebellion against Him and all He stands for makes me buoyant.  The sense of outrage, disrespect for property.  Worse than losing something valuable:  to actually give it away.

I watch *Paper Moon,* a film that disturbs me deeply. A salesman travels in his old car with the girl he pretends is his daughter. Something about it is very familiar, but I am not sure what. I have never sold Bibles, but my father is a salesman, now that He has left the Air Force. I remember staying in motel rooms along the road. I hate white motel towels, the sight of them nauseates me. I think of motels with cheap bedspreads and I remember scenes from the countryside as we drove past the city limits in His car. Or maybe I remember all those Woolworth oil paintings, the nature scenes of bright red barns and autumn colours that seem to decorate every Ontario motel wall. Not the adornments you preferred, Maman, cross-stitch work on the walls, hand-embroidered towels, plaques that read *Home Sweet Home.*

I am afraid that you will die if I tell the truth. I am always protecting you. You only see what you desire, and then your shields arise. Easier to be helpless and defensive. I tell you I want to take an auto mechanics course in case my car breaks down. *Hah,* you laugh, *I would just stick my leg out and wait for some man to help me.* Maybe some women can't rely on that method, I suggest. *They could if women over here took better care to make themselves attractive,* you retort, as if it were unnatural to do otherwise. You giggle and look at me conspiratorially, a sneer of superiority. *Well, at least we don't have to worry about that, do we?* How can I deny your beauty without wounding myself? You are not weak, though. You control everything to your advantage. When you get fat, you join a fitness club, change your lifestyle as easily as you change bedclothes. There is only one thing you cannot find it in your heart to change: your response to me.

My task: to bring back your broomstick.

Maman, why do I feel attracted to people who cannot possibly love me, trying to make the blind see, the cold feel, the unemotional respond to me? The sheer impossibility of holding on to them. The men I choose are challenges to the heart, never suited to me, never kind and giving. I look for small triumphs, trying to get through to them, trying to convert them to my faith, as if trying to convince myself that there would be warmth and touch and love in the world if only I can make them feel something for me. The indifference of my lovers stimulates my obsession with love like a drug, leaving me weak on self-loathing, my veins full of glass shards. I sabotage every relationship I have. Easier that way, to end it myself, rather than see him leave me for someone else. I know that is what they will all do anyway. I expect nothing, so nothing can hurt me. *Nothing lasts forever.* Men like this coldness, they tell me. So many women keep trying to tie them down, to hook them. *See, no hooks here, no strings attached.*

Maman, you give me a book entitled *I Cannot Forgive,* that is about the holocaust, filled with graphic details of mass murders inside gas chambers. I am terrified, ask you if it really happened like that. What do you think people do to deserve it? *Nothing.*

I have your confirmation picture in my photo album, you look so young and convincing, pensive, about to convert from the rituals of ice to the warm soft glow of offertory candles. It used to be perched on my desk, but your eyes followed me continually, everywhere I went, distorted glass eyes that seemed to see all yet stared blindly ahead, seeing nothing. The pupils are glazed over by the glossy finish, the light falls harshly against your cheekbones, capturing your remoteness. I look at myself in the mirror sometimes, and for a moment, before I turn away, I think there is something of you imprisoned in my face; it catches me by surprise. I cannot touch you, cannot really see you. In the mirror I sense I have inherited your self-loathing, want to cast it away, let it shatter. Sometimes I think I see you standing in front of me. I recognize the mask-like face, the clenched teeth, the cruel, battered lines around the corners of your mouth, the clenched teeth and the quivering chin. I want to shake you by the shoulders, slap you hard in the face, wake you out of your somnambulism, point to that invisible umbilical cord and twist it until it bleeds. Just so that I might sense something, make you feel me. But then I am defeated. The violence of such a gesture is already too much yours, the accompanying tone would be something like, *Listen to me, young lady!*

I am in terror of my sister committing suicide, convinced it will happen one day, dream of it constantly and wake up shuddering. I cannot prevent it, am guilty already with the weight of foreknowledge. In one of the memory pictures of her, she is in the twin bed across from mine, watching me stand up and urinate all over my sheets. *Why are you doing that?* My sisters gather about me in my dreams, twisted Harpies chanting one octave above the other, *Why don't you just be normal? Why are you trying to wreck our family? You're always trying to hurt Maman, just when she is finally getting better.*

I dream again of my sister calling to me from the floor below, where she is sitting in an interrogation room. She speaks quietly about what He did to her. I want to run down and embrace her for her bravery, but I do not know how to get to the next floor, even though there is a rope connecting us at the solar plexus. I run up and down the corridor in confusion.

I want to tell her that I remember how we all went to the hospital with her when she kept putting stones up her nose; pebbles from the sandbox kept finding their way into her ears and mouth until she choked. I watched her do it deliberately, selecting the perfect pebble and slowly twisting it into her orifices, a look of concentrated anger on her face. Maman, you never understood that none of this was accidental, only complained that your middle one had a funny sense of humour, your embarrassment at returning to the hospital as palpable as summer humidity. It makes a good story for the relatives, but you forget that I watched her do these things. There is no such thing as an accident.

In the sermon He reads, the garments of Christ are divided by lots after the die are thrown. I can picture this exactly, I understand the game, they divide my clothes after the poker game too, or sometimes play Spin the Bottle. One of them is Mr. Wilson. Another one is very old, as old as my grandfather, and He always turns the bottle toward me, pretending it is an accident. I complain that He is cheating. They tell me that if I do not co-operate and play the game, I will be punished, and He rubs at his belt meaningfully. I know what that means, so I take off my undershirt without another word. This game is no fun anymore. I am nearly naked now, and there is something soft underneath me, a rug that feels like my dog's fur. I pretend I am cuddling my dog.

I am the black sheep now; even my sisters spurn me. He hangs up, His voice controlled when my sisters cry and you look puzzled, Maman: *Forget her.* But all of you forgot me long ago; I am the mistake in the family slide show, a character who slipped into the edges of the frame at the beginning of a chronology long since altered, the illusion of the happy group complete except for one pair of frantic eyes. You have the family priest celebrate mass in your home, the drawing together of family in prayer, the Family Circle menu plan, dinner for four is perfect. I would make it odd. Do you ever think of setting an extra place at the table for me, Maman? Do you ever slip up and accidentally remove one too many plates from the cupboard in your haste?

How I long for the velvet illusion that you really loved me but felt trapped, economically disadvantaged because you had no vocation except marriage. We were poor at first, until He made His way up the company ladder, salesman of the year twice over. You could not work, stuck at home with three young children. Where could you have run to, how could you have supported me?

*A mother always loves her child.* Somewhere you must be hiding your love for me, your heart wrapped under furs. You are a victim, you are excused, you give excuses, but nothing rings true. All these lies collapse like cardboard kettles, splashing me with boiling water; I feel my skin turning raw and then I am overtaken by a slow, kind numbness.

We drive in the company car, in open country. He pushes his body against the steering wheel, buttocks high, straining to remove the handkerchief from his trouser pocket. He leans back into the seat to unzip His fly. *The puppy's nose is all wet again, He needs attention, can you wipe it up? Don't worry, your mother does this for me all the time. Just hold the handkerchief like this.* This time I start crying, watching Him jerk back and forth on the car seat, the creak of metal springs and His low moaning. What makes me cry is not His shouting at me, but the sight of the little blue monogrammed A at the edge of the handkerchief. It is wet and crumpled, and He doesn't even notice it. My feelings are hurt. My birthday gift to Him.

The city is an eerie dreamscape, trees and storefront facades tower over me like giants, tall office buildings scrutinize me like the Cyclops, threatening to reveal my secrets. Their menace surprises me when I visit the city several years later, having seen the historic and great cities of Europe, against which this city is humbled. In the dream, I run down the streets. Years later, I come "home" to the city, and am shocked to observe how modest in height the buildings actually are, how safe and artificially pretty the downtown facades appear. The sight of a familiar limestone building fills me with inexplicable relief; it must be some kind of landmark. Every route is filled with dread, invested with nightmares, so that I cannot stroll down the main street without feeling dizzy with guilt and memory, overwhelmed with fear. Ordinary city, smug.

I drive down Highbury Avenue, to the ice cream store and playground where we used to stop every Sunday after mass. It is no longer called the Dairy Dell, but Shaw's; it has been cleaned up and there is no playground with tree fort or swings or whirl-a-round. *Whirleypuke,* He called it. I feel sick anyway, close to gagging, tense. The only time I relax is when I see the highway exit, the way out. Where I used to stand with my thumb out, looking for escape. There is the post office on the edge of town, where He once made me get out of the car. I refused to co-operate that time; it was a nice day and I didn't mind walking. The sight of that single-story structure I equate with a glorious freedom and the taste of highway grit in my mouth.

I dissect frogs in my biology class. The teacher demonstrates how it is done: make a slit down the belly, then two more above and below, so the skin can be peeled back, opened like a window shutter. I do not mind this part. When the pins are pierced through the flaps of skin, I feel a sharp pain in my groin, the opening of each window shutter exposes pain and grizzly innards. I run out of the classroom, vomit seeping through my clenched teeth.

Tonight I remember this, it comes back to me in a cold and sweaty dream, the clamminess of exposed skin, dead tissue. On my vulva appear inexplicable small dots of blood, red gooseflesh bumps. My period is not due for two weeks. A variation on the stigmata of Christ; maybe I am achieving holiness at last? I run to the bathroom, turn on the fluorescent light, look again, and blood spots are still there. What is happening to me?

*I don't want you to move. This will only sting a little bit. This way you will have to stay awake until I am ready for you. If you think this hurts, imagine how much better it will feel when I take them out. The more you move, the more they will stick into you. So you better stay still and be quiet like I tell you.*

While I am away at school, again you sneak into my room and open the locked drawer to my dresser, where I keep my diary. You read that I feel suicidal, that I have tried drugs, stolen a bottle from the liquor cabinet and been drunk with my friends after cutting classes one afternoon. You find birth control pills in neat packages between my underwear, love letters from people whom you will never know. All of these things you reveal to me one day in a rage. I am too shocked to feel defensive, to deny the charges you heap on me. Privacy is sacred, you always told me that, I was not to come into your room without knocking first. What was it you wanted to know about me? Why were you spying on me all those years?

Maman, you tell me I need to go on a diet, you pack a can of tuna and dry toast in cellophane for my lunch. I eat this in the privacy of the bathroom stall at school, reading the graffiti on the back of the door. I am embarrassed. When I get off the bus at the corner store on the way home from school, I buy bags of broken chocolate bars at Kresge's, consume them hungrily in the seclusion of the alleyway. You say it is because you care about me, that I need more self-respect. And this is why you give me nothing but a lime green jogging suit for Christmas, promises of new clothes once I lose weight. I hate green; it is the colour of humiliation. Green is my ugly inner self, the one no one is ever allowed to see. She is shy and awkward, and she is impossible to love.

Maman, you see *The Exorcist* and have another nervous breakdown, describe yourself as possessed, relieved that you have finally found a name for it. My uncle comes to take you away this time; later he tells us over dinner that you refused to let go of the huge marble crucifix above your bed, tore it from the hinges, pulling plaster flakes onto the new bedspread.

I watch you prepare the feast. The first day, you do all the shopping. The second day is for marinating, for shaping the pâté, doing all the baking. And on the third day, the finishing touches. You rise early on the day of the dinner and go through all your recipes once more. Around the dinner table, in front of the guests, He apologizes for you. *It's too salty. She usually cooks better than this.* You cringe, apologize. My anger at your forced humility fills my chest and I choke on my water. I want to defend you, shout at Him that He is being unfair. I love your food, Maman.

I write to an older convent girl who sings in the church choir with me on Sundays. It is not safe to write in my diary anymore, because you always read it. I send Smarties to this girl, I think I may be in love. She always thanks me for these letters at choir practice every Wednesday night, I watch and admire the way she sparkles when she plays the guitar. You find me mailing one of my letters one day. Your mouth grows tight, you say nothing. But next Saturday, when we are downtown, you spit out your words angrily. *She is a lesbian. How dare you talk with her?*

I have always admired tough, athletic women, chosen them as my friends, because they seemed invincible, invulnerable, everything I was not. I model myself after them, learn to dress tough, wear golf shirts and sweat pants. I walk with hunched shoulders, or swagger with upraised shoulders, hiding my breasts, hoping they will disappear from view, that no one will grab them from behind, or poke at them the way He does. *Hey, hey, getting to be a little woman now, eh? Just teasing you. Can't you take a joke?*

I have taken up sewing with several of the girls in our church; we are working on a quilt under the supervision of the choirmaster's wife. He does not approve of these "make-work" sessions. *Stitch n' Bitch sessions. A bunch of old gossips with nothing else to do.* He would rather I was at home, He says I am needed, that there are my sisters to look after while you are in the hospital, Maman. But I love the quiet hum in the church basement as we work, the way the light animates the dust motes in the room in the late afternoon sun, how our needles catch the light.

I sleep with many men, many women, in my determination to have a normal sex life.    I can remember almost nothing of this phase of my life, except that I go to bed with anyone who asks me.  A smorgasbord of lovers, but no feelings, no garnish. *Each one teaches me something. At least I have no hangups about possessiveness, I regret none of my encounters.*  These are the words I use to justify the sense of emptiness inside.  Sometimes I let myself be used.  I allow myself to feel nothing.  I am too open and vulnerable, but I tell no one.  I can barely remember their names.  Only that great numbness, over and over.  I survive.  I owe this much to you, Maman, your first catechism to me: *If you fall off a horse, you must get up and ride Him again right away, let Him know who is boss.*

At a party, I smoke pot and drop acid, drink too much, pass out.  I wake up to see the sun pushing through the shutters.  There is a hole in my skin just above the wrist, the bone is peeking through the red tissue, curtains of flesh peeling back.  The smell of something burning.  Later a joker tells me he held a cigarette to me because I claimed I never felt any pain, that I was indestructible, that he was just testing me.

119

Today I called one of the nuns at the convent where you sent me. *The house on the hill for wayward girls.* Run by the penguin patrol, black and white nuns who herd the girls together. It stuns me the day they all take their veils off; under their habits are real women. One is named Sister St. Xavier; she is now eighty-two years old. She asks me if I still play the piano. No, I say slowly, guiltily. She says that she thought I had great depth, sensitivity, that this is what inspired the sisters to give me free music lessons. I am aghast. Free? One of His ploys was to make me feel indebted for my piano lessons. *Costing me a goddam fortune. You better deserve them. Get up those stairs now, young lady, and start practising.* What stays with me after this revelation is not outrage against Him, but sadness that no one had ever told me I had any musical gift. I might have continued practising, might have dreamed . . .

I am a rebel, and the convent affords the perfect environment for my acts of rebellion. The only nun I trust is named Sister Marie-Françoise, and she has just taken off her veil, so I do not even think of her as a nun. I tell her about my family situation. But even she betrays me, repeats everything to the Mother Superior who contacts you immediately.

One of my classmates tells me that I am unfit for athletics, because my head is too small for my torso, that I am ill-proportioned. I try to compensate for this by developing my head. I cease playing sports, ashamed of my ungainly body.

Summer arrives and I can escape my convent uniform, put it away in dry-cleaner's plastic and mothballs. I have a summer job that gets me away from home. There is a man at the day camp where I am a counsellor in training, in charge of the recreation program. He writes sensitive poems about seagulls being trapped in oil, speaks passionately against pollution. I think he has come to release me. He understands my thoughts, does not laugh at me. One night I drop acid and I am afraid. I call him at home; I have looked up his phone number in the phone book many times, obsessed with the idea of being rescued, the number memorized like a chant from the hit parade repeating over and over again in my brain. He makes me feel safe. I am tired, cold, hungry. He feeds me, then gives me a bath. He shaves in the mirror. After he wraps me in his bathrobe, takes me to his bed and begins masturbating me. *I want to show you that you can feel good without having sex.* I am confused. He laughs and calls me his Little Leda.

121

At last I move out, pack my belongings in a suitcase and fling it into a taxi on the night you have left me in charge of dispensing Hallowe'en treats. Slowly I turn out the lights, extinguish the pain of the house itself. I move into a room in a boarding house, across from Victoria Park. At night I can hear the people in the room beside me fighting, a woman keeps screaming. With my first pay cheque from the Y, I buy ear plugs. I am enormously happy to be on my own. And it pleases me that you do not know my address. Only one message from you arrives through my aunt: *Return the suitcase immediately. It belongs to a set.*

I spend a lot of time hiking. I make lists of survival gear. The first pieces of equipment I purchase when I leave home are a tent and a backpack. It makes me feel secure to know that I am going to be prepared, even if I do not find a home. I will be totally self-sufficient, eat from my mess kit, be able to live in the woods for weeks at a time if necessary. I need no one. A simple lifestyle is the best.

I am happy in my room in the boarding house until the owners evict everyone on the grounds that renovations to the building are necessary. I have no money, so I roam the streets. Because I am a minor, the police bring me back to your house, Maman. You are very polite with them, explain that you have done all you can. *As you can see, Officer, she has a good home.*

There is a man named Roger who is coming to fetch me in a few hours. I met him in a bar one night, and he has been terribly kind to me. I feel excited: I am going to live with a man. I have brought cardboard boxes home from the corner grocery store, and I spend all morning packing my clothes and books. I stand at the back door, waiting while you pace, Maman. I realize, after he is two hours late, that he lied. He will not come to get me after all. Where will I go now? You tell me that if I walk out that door, I can never come home again. *You made your bed, you lie in it.* I call a taxi and leave.

No place to go.  No money.  Forced back home.  Silences. Colourless and empty.  Round and round we go.  Who will listen to me anyway?  I have been told that I come from a normal family.  You tell us we are better off than most, better than others.  The priest reminds us how fortunate we are.  Until I leave your house, Maman, I continue to believe this.  Now I am preparing for another journey, packing my bags.  It is not until I arrive in the cold country of the Snow Queen, where you send me to live with your mother, that I realize nothing is at all ordinary about where I come from.

I am standing beside my suitcase, my teddy bear stuffed inside at the last minute. *You have disgraced all of us.* I am fourteen years old. I am possessed by a demon. What is happening to my body? Every morning for the last three weeks I throw up, drag myself down to the breakfast table. My skirts no longer fit where my belly has begun to swell. Is this why you are sending me to the old country to live with my grandmother? What have I done now? *Maudite putain. You have brought this family nothing but shame since the day you were born.* Your eyes penetrate me, violate me with your knowledge. I do not understand what is happening to me. Sometimes I cry all day. Sometimes I sleep like the dead.

Maman, Maman, *why hast thou forsaken me?*

In my grandmother's garden there is a bush with red berries. They are especially brilliant in contrast with the blinding white snow on the ground, lurid in their opulence next to the austerity of rows so rigidly designed that they maintain their structured outlines even under the weight of snow. I dream at night that I have lost my red wooden shoes, and must travel barefoot in my search for you, Maman. On winter mornings, waking in a cold sweat, I throw open the sash from my window and watch snowflakes grow into a regiment of fantastic shapes whose glittering white purity is unmistakable. Your mother looks like the sea witch, and she makes me special potions so that I can survive the pain of my heartache, the growing girth of my belly. She pinches my skin with pearls, and tells me over and over again that it takes great pain to be beautiful.

*Ssh,* says my grandmother, *I will help you raise your child. It will be our little secret. No one will know.* But the devil inhabits my body, this much I know. I have seen the evidence. I have prayed for Rosemary's baby. Satan governs all. I feel Him moving around in my belly in the middle of the night.

How is it that I have no recollection of this birth, have wiped all residue of memory from my mind?  As if it never happened; as if my body were frozen and clamped into place and something pried away from between my thighs.  There are no cries, no pictures, nothing to pin the pain on.

I am fifteen.  I wake up, hungover, and He is laughing in bed beside me.  Who is this man?  The family has approved of Him.  He is kind, older, and most importantly, rich.  This excites me.  He allows me to escape.  Slowly I remember the ceremony, and realize in horror that I am actually married to the grizzled face of the old man on the pillow beside me.  He has adopted my child, and now we are playing house.  He is better at it than I am, and takes good care of the baby. After six weeks of marriage, I leave Him, and the child who could never be mine, for Paris.

I come back across the Atlantic, after two years' absence. You do not say you love me, you do not say you are sorry. Instead: *All is forgiven. We have a surprise for you.* Daddy has started his own business. He has gained a fortune. All of your dreams have come true. There is a new swimming pool in the backyard, visible from my bedroom window. You have remodelled my bedroom, so that I no longer recognize anything. The summer sun plays on the artificial turquoise water. I am dazzled, but something hurts. You have always given obligations, not gifts. I do not trust this gift either.

One of the conditions you have made for my returning home is that I am supposed to attend school, and then rush to my part-time job. Instead I drift through the park, anticipating inspiration. I shoplift, steal everything I can. I spend hours downtown, avoiding people. I do not care if I am caught, secretly hope that someone will notice that I am taking what you never gave me. I steal costume jewellery, clothing. I want someone to feel sorry for me, as I stuff sirloin steak packages down my overalls, the cellophane cold and clammy next to my bare skin. At night I dream of stealing whole houses, fantasies as sharp as if I'd already committed the crime. I eat compulsively for hours, tasting nothing, filling my mouth, blocking my throat so that the screams will not emerge. I dream of mountains of food, endless closets of beautiful clothes, a pair of shoes for every day of the week.

It is too much. I have to get my own place again. I find a shared apartment on the wrong side of the tracks.

I have come home to visit you after a long absence, Maman. The family priest and guests are all invited to dinner. Before supper I go upstairs to be alone, but He corners me in the room. *I want to make up for everything.* I am terrified by the look in His eyes, hate the smell of beer on His breath, it overpowers me. I turn from Him, but He grabs my arm, twists it behind me, and marches me into the living room, where He addresses all of the guests. *Look at how dilated her pupils are. What should we do with this girl? What are we supposed to do with a girl who insists on taking drugs after we tell her never to come home in this state? She has broken her word again.* In disgust, He pushes me toward the door. There is an embarrassed silence in the living room until polite conversation resumes.

*Thou art my hiding place; thou shalt preserve me from trouble; thou shalt compass me about with songs of deliverance.* You are driving me back to my apartment in your fancy car, when you stop at a gas station. I watch you open your hood for the attendant to check your oil. He removes the rod, and the oil rolls down in viscous clots like blood, like tears, like wax on the offertory candles in front of the statue of the Virgin Mary. That night I dream that I hear all the guests throwing up behind the bathroom door before coming back down to the dinner table.

Maman, I think of you most of all when the wall between madness and reality collapses. One of my first nervous breakdowns happens when I am alone in my apartment. I call you over after not having slept for two nights; I have been living on coffee and bennies and raw nerves. I am going over the edge, something inside me has cracked, and I lie on my bed crying for hours without knowing why I feel so badly. There are random pictures that keep returning to the surface of my consciousness, sparks from some other lifetime, but none of it makes sense to me. You always come in a hurry when I am failing. You enter the tiny living room and immediately sense the significance of my chaos, see the dead moth lying on the middle of the floor and realize why I am crying. I believe I have killed a butterfly. *I didn't mean to do it, it was an accident, it just got in the way.* Hysterical ramblings, the magnificent symbolic proportions of my murderous act.

133

I let myself be seduced, abused, abandoned. I am used to pain, its familiarity comforts me. I am trying to find out the truth, trying to find out what I can feel. I feel nothing. Pain darts out of the solar plexus like a quivering arrow, making me nauseous. Not Cupid's arrows, these tremors. Devil's daggers, for the tormented in Hell.

I eat compulsively for hours, then starve myself for days. I spend a lot of time considering the sharpness of razor blades. I want to feel something. *Lead us not into temptation.* In my blood, I know that depression is merely withheld knowledge that somehow must reveal itself.

Maman, Maman, *why hast thou forsaken me?*

Once more I move. I am going nowhere. I have a tiny basement apartment with six other girls; it is dark and crowded. Sometimes I do not come back because I feel depressed whenever I walk through the door. One night when no one else is there, I swallow three bottles of sleeping pills after drinking a bottle of gin. In the hospital, I am force-fed emetics, in spite of my resistance, and they make me throw up. I am angry that my plan did not work, that my roommate came back to find me collapsed on the floor. But the worst part is that He is waiting there to take me home again; His face is the first thing I see when I wake up.

When I leave home for the final time, I am as defiant as the little girl who once stood up in her bed and wet the sheets each night in protest, trying to ward off the devil with my foul human smell. I take a new name now, Liza. Elizabeth was your name for me, Maman, *oath of God.* I leave it behind, in all its submissive timidity and soft sibilance, the burden of too many syllables.

I try to slash my wrists, but the sight of blood makes me sick. I try an overdose. I will try anything, just not to be here. It is gray outside the window. Nothing else remains in my memory of this whole year. A hospital room. A bed. The ghosts of memory.

I get out after one year and two months. I am working at two jobs and attending school full-time during the day, living on bennies and coffee and two hours of sleep a night. On Saturdays I do laundry and shopping; on Sundays I catch up on my sleep. I also work weekends cleaning houses for rich people. One woman tries to get to know me, asks me about my family. I say I am an orphan, that my mother and father were killed in a car accident so long ago that I cannot remember.

Today, fifteen years later, I receive a copy of my psychiatric assessment, which I requested my doctor to obtain for me many months ago. In it you are described as a caring mother, sincere, concerned, at your wit's end. My suicide attempts, all eighteen of them, are described as manipulative and "typically adolescent."

*Babies are things men impose on you, to force you away from doing anything else, so you can't ask them to love you as much.* For most of my life I really believe your words, Maman; I remain convinced that babies are inflicted on women to keep them trapped and submissive. But when I write to tell you that I have convinced a doctor to tie my tubes, you are irate. *How terrible that you will never see the features of the man you love imprinted on your child's face.* This is in your letter that my friend hands to me when I wake from my operation, still lost in a stuporous fog. My anger increases with consciousness. No matter what you say, no devil will ever come into my body again, no parasite will ever live off it. How strongly I want to be different from you, not to be trapped, hindered. I will never be like you; I will be free, have a career, dependent on no one but myself; no man will ever control me.

And now years later, I carry your portrait in my heart, engraved in the metal of my mind, the only features I never wanted to keep, indelibly preserved.

I am reading over all these journal entries and none of them makes sense. Some are in different handwriting styles. I do not recognize myself. Certain passages are so angry, I know that Red has taken over, that angry bitch. I have no photos of myself as a child, only the black and white picture of me holding the hand of my little sister. And the one of my old terrier by the side of the swimming pool, the only friend to greet me upon my return from the old country.

Why am I writing to you at all? I know now that you will never answer. Inside me there is a little girl who continually overestimates you, who remains an incurable optimist. She speaks to me constantly. I am forever repentant; I just cannot remember what it is you want me to be sorry for. The numbly repeated words, ritual incantations that guarantee you will like me again for a couple of hours. But that is not why I have come back here at all. I came to see if you felt anything for me yet, Maman. Family Reunion. He introduces me to my sisters and aunts and uncles after all these unexplained years. And how did you excuse my absence during that time, when the neighbourhood matrons invited you to their daughters' weddings, their pool parties? *We are sorry to announce the disappearance of our eldest daughter on a trip to El Salvador.* Make it official, formal. *A political misunderstanding beyond our control. We think she was into drugs. Sold on the slave market.* The delicious incongruity between your stories of me and the truth, the lie and the flesh.

I am suspended from school. Suspended, in mid-air. I work as a waitress in a downtown restaurant, and take correspondence courses to complete high school. I get a student loan and study for a B.A. in English Literature. I turn twenty-one. All this without you.

The telegram arrives just before my final exam. The child I bore in the Ice Country is dead, killed in a bus and train collision while on a school trip. The words on the page are foreign, remind me of another lifetime that seems far too distant now. For days I walk in a fog of despair and disbelief. All those years when the man I married cared for her; I had nothing to do with her upbringing. Even her funeral arrangements are taken from me; I am given no control. Red's anger is beyond her normal level as she forces me to walk in the woods and howl at the trees. My world is reduced to the collision of metal and flesh. Then Green's voice penetrates my mind. *I am a lousy mother. I am no good; she would never have died if it were not for me. If I had been there, it would never have happened. If. If.*

I will never recover this time.

A friend of mine tries to get too close and I lash out at her, I hit her across the face with my full hand. It is Red again. Why do I sabotage every effort at intimacy, why am I so afraid? She was only trying to be kind to me.

I inherit my grandfather's sofa. Pépé died last week. Maman, you make me go to the funeral. Odd that none of my cousins is in tears either. I am dry-eyed, cold. Wanting to get back to my reading, a detective story. I spend nearly all my time reading mystery novels, I am looking for the perfect crime, I curl up in the corner with my feet tucked under the cushions. Now my relatives think they are helping out a poor student, but I cannot read on this sofa, I feel sick. Two weeks later, I give it away. Maman, you noticed right away. *Ungrateful, picky, aren't we?* I tell you I think it is too ugly, that I cannot bear to look at it any more. Actually it is the smell, musty and foreboding, faint odour of armpits, or something I cannot quite put my finger on.

*You would make a good actress, because you can lie so well, you are so good at pretending and make-believe.* He has always told me this. Now I am acting in a play called *The Crucible* at the university theatre. There are a lot of hysterical women, the director says. My role is to lie prone in bed until I hear my cue and then start screaming. I am surprised at how convincing I am at this. The man who plays my New England father is my English professor. Hysteria spreads; one woman's account of witchcraft prompts another's; soon everyone on the stage is screaming. Emotionalism. We are repressed, the director says. But this is easy, it spreads like wildfire; I can see the other girls are finding it infectious too, the terror on their faces is so real I forget this is a play.

I receive a scholarship. I get into graduate school. I look pleased to be winning the game. I think about beating Him, about going to law school and suing Him, humiliating Him in public. But at night I lie in bed and know that I deserve none of this good fortune, and soon someone will discover my fraudulence and take everything away. *I am going to give you a big slap if you don't shut up right now. That's for nothing. Imagine if I gave you what you really deserved.*

I am still afraid of basements, dark places. The smell of mildew makes me want to gag. I try to live in a basement apartment to save money, but there are ghosts there; I usually go to the corner restaurant for coffee because I fear I will not be able to fall asleep. I do not understand why I have this illogical fear of basements and root cellars. In a strange house, I always prop chairs in front of the cellar door before I let myself go to sleep on the living room couch. In one apartment, there is a ghost who sits at the end of my bed and smokes, watches me when I am trying to go to sleep. I can feel His breath on my face.

I am reading Virginia Woolf, and some memory splits me open like overripe fruit. Not now. Postpone introspection until it is safe. I still have two term papers to write this week. I feel the weight of the stone in her pocket: it is my unborn child, my silent self, my heart of heaviness. And I wade into the water with Virginia at my side, holding my hand.

I wake up screaming, feel hot flashes in my womb, my solar plexus throbbing. For years I have chronic abdominal pains. This is diagnosed as hysteria; a doctor recommends a hysterectomy. Once I am delivered to the hospital in a similar condition, but they send me home after removing my appendix. Yet the unidentifiable pulsing pains remain. Another time they suggest I am neurotic, that I see a psychiatrist about my overreacting. In graduate school when I appear repeatedly in the emergency ward, I am sent home and warned about stress, told that I risk an ulcer. Something is burning in my esophagus, and I feel like I have to swallow over and over again.

I forget to eat or to wash for days. It is just a body, after all. Scrub it away in the shower.

I am giving a seminar presentation. I feel like Alice, disappearing down the rabbit hole. It is too dangerous to stand up and speak, the audience keeps growing further and further away, diminishing in size. I open my mouth to speak, and nothing comes out. At first I cannot believe it, I have practised reading this paper several times. But now there is a lump at the back of my throat, the taste is salty, I cannot breathe. What is wrong? I do not lack confidence; this is a good paper. My jaw locks and I am forced to sit down. *Don't you dare say a word. No one will ever believe anything you say, you are a worthless little bitch.* When I try to speak, the words are trapped like hot lava below the surface. Something is about to burst, like a pimple under pressure. My jaw remains locked.

I make an appointment to see a speech therapist, ask her for exercises to help me unlock my jaw. I see her for one year and work on relaxing my throat, getting Him out of my mouth. I also enroll in a public speaking class to gain confidence and to help erase the voices in my head that tell me I can never open my mouth about anything.

I long to sing. *O hear the angels' voices.* Even though I hear sweet harmonies in my mind, mere grunts emerge when I open my mouth.

In graduate school, I write essays about divided artists, about the *doppelgänger*. I consume Russian fiction voraciously. I specialize in fiction about insanity, madness, schizophrenic states. I do not know what my attraction is to these works.

I cannot stomach anything at school, the way my professors look at me. I rush home immediately after class and eat while I read all night: pizza, chocolate, keilbossa, cheese and Ritz crackers, even though I loathe these foods. Food is endowed with mystical significance, and if I keep eating the appropriate symbolic foods in the right proportions, I will begin to understand, I will fill the black hole inside of me that threatens to engulf me. Where do these cravings come from? Eating seems the most forbidden, dangerous activity I can indulge in, as if by eating through layers and layers of memory, I can somehow get closer to you, Maman. I have an uncontrollable and overwhelming greed. There are two choices: I can go mad, and end up back in the hospital with all the other loonies; or I can get mad, go and kill him, and end up in jail. I want to run back home. But where is home? Home means danger. There is no one who can give me what I need.

When I teach a self-defense class, I tell the students that they must think of someone who angers them in order to direct their punches. His eyes, His groin, are my targets, especially in my dreams where I am a Zen archer with perfect aim, or a baseball star, the back of His skull cracking with a whack as I hit the ball and run freely from base to base.

I think about having a baby of my own, a compulsion as real as hunger, but sharp with danger. I make an appointment with the clinic; several months later, I am having surgery to reverse my tubal ligation, after ten years of being held in knots. One tube cannot be restored. Only fifty per cent chance of conception. Recovering from the operation in the hospital ward, I am dazzled by the snowflakes piling up on the windowsill.

152

At last this illusion is over, Maman. I disclose the truth to you. I make an appointment two weeks in advance to see you, and I cannot eat or study during this period; I keep rehearsing what I will say to you. Nervously I await the arrival of your car outside my window. We decide to go out. The only place open is a cheap restaurant, where they charge a dollar for each cup of coffee if you do not order food. Of course neither of us does. You are still aghast at the exorbitant cost; years of economizing have not allowed you to adjust to your new wealth, His wealth; normally you would leave politely after one cup, but you let the waitress keep filling your thick porcelain mug. You say nothing, smoke cigarette after cigarette. But in the car your words are harsh and considered. You would hit me if you did not have to keep your hands on the steering wheel, gripping the leather. Don't you recognize me, your errant Cordelia, the only one to denounce the lies, waiting for her mother's benediction? Reach down and touch me, this is my own hair, no sheepskin disguise. *Whore. Liar. Are you trying to ruin my marriage? You would always do anything to get attention, but you have gone too far this time, do you hear me. Why should He want you when He has me?*

What was I expecting, that you would lean down from your saddle, swoop me up and gallop off into the sunset with me? Secretly I long for some dramatic gesture. Instead your only concern is your own desirability. Maman, can't you see I have never stopped desiring you? My loneliness is reinforced by the blackness of a starless night, a night with no memory of the day. Even the stars, distortions of intense light, utterly reject me. Or maybe I simply cannot see them anymore.

I have a new job as a journalist. I distrust my boss; she is cold and distant. She reminds me of you, Maman. Always judging, always taking notes, telling me to work harder. Her voice is as harsh and shrill as the Editor's. I try to make her like me, but it is never possible, *I am not good enough.* She will never accept me. I think she is jealous of me. Grudgingly she tells me one day that I have spunk, but I do not know if she means this as a compliment or not. She searches my face for signs, clues. Like rifling through dresser drawers. And I want her to find the pieces, put them together. I have a dream where I take her to my attic. But as we approach the top floor, she excuses herself and says she has to attend a meeting. She ignores the picture of the Sacred Heart that hangs on the wall, beseeching her with pleading eyes, dripping blood on the stairs.

I have found a new partner.

I am pregnant again. The baby is mine this time. I miss you these days, Maman, especially since I am travelling in a country where mothers hold their babies to their breasts on their daily pilgrimages to the market. On other days I feel omnipotent, huge and grateful. This longing for you stretches across my heart like Ariadne's thread, our visceral connection, the longing to be entwined in the twin spiralling arms of love, the curvature of space beyond infinity. I want you to speak to me before I lose the end of the thread, my dreams unwinding like entrails used in sacrificial rituals. Greek statues remind me of you when I am touring the Peloponnesus, I see you smiling benignly at me. At Corinth, I seek relief from the heat and dust, and sit down on a huge rock, disturbing a snake that has coiled herself around the stone. I think of you all the time. My love and my rage are internalized, I inflict guilt over you upon myself, dance circles around your heart in order to spare you further pain.

When I lie in bed at night and feel the suffocating ghostweight of Him on top of me, I shriek in pain for you, Maman. *Whatsoever they do to the least of my sisters.* Every rape I read about in the paper also happens to me, a series of unending rapes. I cannot separate pain anymore, outer or inner. I feel all events too deeply. I read in the newspaper of a little boy who is run over by a bus and I weep for days, the sadness slowly fading into fatigue. I cannot tell anymore where I end and someone else begins, there are only scattered pieces of everyone, all mixed up. It is all my fault. I find it impossible to say no to anyone, am afraid of hurting anyone's feelings.

I become more and more like you, Maman, programmed against my will. The mirror speaks back to me. I do not know if what happened to me also happened to you, to my sisters, if the whole world is being slowly fucked to death and, politely, no one mentions it. We are all being ripped apart, but we never speak of such things. Every telephone pole wounds the sky, wires split like fallopian tubes being pulled in opposing directions, piercing clouds that are soft and white with the promise of spring.

He raises His glass in a toast. I have returned home for the first time after endless years. *To the prodigal daughter, who has come back to atone for her errors.* You raise your glass as well, Maman, and my sisters join in hesitantly. I am not drinking, I say, I am pregnant. I am astonished that the anger can course through my veins and fuel my emotions so palpably. The hairs on my arms are on end. But we are all so polite. *You should join in the toast, anyway.* He pushes a glass toward me menacingly. *After all, we are welcoming you back to the flock.* Small titter at the religious allusions. It is true I am the prodigal daughter, but not in the way He implies. I have given too much of my personal fortune to the wrong people, I think to myself. This satisfies me, I drink, your eyes across the table signal approval, Maman. Of course, you do not know what I think.

During my pregnancy, I eat ice cream every day, compulsively, with a vague sense of guilt. Required calcium, I tell myself. I cannot drink milk, which sticks in my throat like phlegm. No, like something else, a deeper guilt. Whenever I am sad, I eat ice cream, even in the winter. I am certain it will be a boy, use the pronoun he without hesitation. I dream of being trapped in a subterranean dungeon, unable to escape. I am ravenously hungry. I am looking for you, seeking your lap, depressed, guilty. Thoughts of you come tumbling down the corridor of memory, your face written in the cumulus clouds that follow me overhead. If only I could decipher the picture, the hidden symbols you left there for me.

I give you a second chance to come and rescue me, Maman. Come and attend the birth of this child, my child, this time. *Of course I will be there.* All through my pregnancy I long for you, for your reassurances, your advice; even old wives' tales, though disbelieved, would be welcome. I hope you will come and guide me. Help me to get the little one out. I am still waiting. You never come. I feel deserted, collapsed from within, contradicted by my enormous belly. My heart beats in time with the small fists that knock against my uterus, in anxiety and disbelief.

Maman, Maman, *why hast thou forsaken me?*

I will give birth to a boy this time, I convince myself, and his name shall be Adonis, a child of great beauty of whom even the gods will be in awe. I can already see him running in the fields. Look at me. I am free. *Mirame.* He is so natural in this setting that he seems to have sprung from a tree, a young sapling bending in the winds. But I must cease these idle reveries, the rich daydreams of pregnant women.

Everything comes to me in lurid colour now. I am giving birth to another daughter. Someone is tinkering with my brain, stimulating the core that revives the emotional context of all those forgotten memories, returning in waves between the peaks of pain. I hear snatches of the lullabies you sang to me, old songs, flooded by the caress of soft breezes in some faraway field. None of this feels connected to the girl who is emerging from between my thighs. I am in a trance in which I can hear you calling to me. Further and further back into that tunnel of memory, I feel myself dragged, sucked backwards in time. If I look back far enough, maybe you will be there. How I long for you standing at the edge of the labour table, holding my hand, soothing me.

It is happening all over again! I have another baby girl, who wakes me up every several hours to nurse. I begin to understand why sleep deprivation is a torture technique: I become a prisoner of forgetfulness, clumsiness, irrationality. Continual interruption, not knowing if I am awake or asleep. My legs are made of rubber, and I am not conscious of moving or walking. The humidity obscures all detail, dropping a heavy veil on perception. Nothing appears as it is. *You are so screwed up. You see everything your own twisted way. How do you expect us to believe you?* My dreams are wild, I am constantly tearful, walking in a trance, my days are hallucinations, one blurring with the next. Nothing is clear anymore. I am trapped in diffused light and cannot find the direct source.

I name her Kassandra. The prophetess whom no one would believe. In the hospital I have been given a coupon for a free portrait of my baby, which I decide would make a nice present for the baby's grandparents. I call the photographer to come to my home, thinking this is a wonderful arrangement, convenient for new and tired mothers. The baby cries for three hours, will not smile to have her photo taken. Two weeks later he arrives with the proofs, and again she starts howling. He then presents his package deals, appeals to my new motherpride, my obligations to relatives. I pay him a large deposit, and he says he will send the photographs in one week. The photos never arrive. Instead I receive obscene phone calls from a man in the middle of the night whose voice is remarkably like the photographer's. I am alone, and I feel invaded again, threatened, vulnerable. I feel sick. First he steals my daughter's spirit between the shutters of his camera, and then he steals my money, my trust, and my peace of mind. I should have listened to my daughter's warning, her instincts were correct. I did not hear her, Maman, as you never heard me. Am I doomed to repeat the same mistakes?

I watch my baby daughter crawl across the floor, and my love for her wells up inside me with the weight of unshed tears. If I thought someone were trying to harm her, I would kill without hesitation, mother bear instinct. I would flee the city with her wrapped in my arms, endure welfare offices and humiliation all over again. There are no exemptions.

I look at my daughter lying beside me in bed, her face angelic in repose. Pure, beautiful, innocent. In her eyes, now slowly opening, shine the jewels of hope and trust. I know from the only picture I have of myself as a baby that she resembles me. I start to cry, wondering why He would want to harm such a small and perfect being, barely one-tenth His size. Green tells me that I am worthless again. I feel deep loneliness, abandonment.

I always believed I was angry only at Him but, with sudden and blinding certainty, I know I shielded you from my rage. Red tells me that she always knew that you were aware of what He was doing when you were lying down in the other room. Nothing He did ever mattered as much as the picture I retain of you that day I walked through the front door of the house with my new friend, the first person to whom I told my story. You had your arms pinned behind

162

you, so that from the front, it appeared you had no limbs at all, that you were helpless, crippled at birth. *I cannot forgive.*

I dream of floating in a canoe among ice floes, do not know where I am headed. All the ice blocks look the same, some might be islands but I have to step on them to find out and then I could drown. I cannot take my bearings and find my way back because everything is the same for miles around, just hunks of ice bobbing up and down. I am cut off from everything, the edges of the ice are as jagged as knives, if I reach out to touch them, they will rip my flesh apart.

In the thick humidity of August, I clean the kitchen early in the morning. I hope to get things in order before the baby is awake. I left the dishrag in the sink overnight, where it lies growing a slimy mold. I pick it up to wring it out, still half asleep, and then drop it screaming. The same viscous matter covers the counter top, oozing from a watermelon left out overnight because it was too large to fit into the refrigerator. I wipe the counter over and over, but the slime will not go away. For the remainder of the day, I feel slime everywhere; it covers everything I touch. I think of the scene from *Moby Dick* where all the crew members wring their hands in spermecetti oil. No communal feeling now, just the sense of being trapped like a fly in viscous ooze. Haunted by dread that *all the perfumes of Arabia will never sweeten.* . . . I lie down for an afternoon nap, and the nightmares come flooding back. The polar bear glass eyes again, brown with a hard glass yellow centre, darker than any of my childhood marbles. I smell something that makes me feel sick. Vanilla, you insisted. But it is semen, a smell I know better than home baking.

A week later, with the same marble eyes staring at me each night in my dreams, the sequence is complete. For several days, I have been haunted by the sound of ice cubes tinkling against glass as I go about my chores. In my dream one night, I am lying on a polar bear skin rug. They are drinking and playing cards. *Come, ye children, hearken unto me: I will teach you the fear of the Lord.* All I can see from this angle is the glass with the ice cubes that they keep tilting in my face. Frighteningly large glass eyes are watching me. *The eyes of the Lord are upon the righteous, and His ears are open unto their cry.* I scream out loud. The pain is unbearable; I cannot breathe; it is very hot down here on the rug with the big body on top of mine; I can only see the dead brown eyes of the bear; evil yellow at the centres, and they are laughing at me. The sharp scent of strong whisky. Ice cubes, flashing gold teeth; cold eyes; hot fur; the pictures are trapped and frozen behind glass; I cannot quite touch them. I dream the same dream over and over again, and each time another detail comes into focus. No faces at first; only the watchful eyes. *The face of the Lord is against them that do evil, to cut off the remembrance of them from the earth.* Every time after I awaken from this dream, I rush to the toilet and vomit.

Today I arrived home from the swimming pool with chewing gum stuck in my hair, and tried to cut it out of my hair with nail scissors. Nothing I could do would mask the fact that a large chunk of my hair was now missing. I take the bus to a salon to have my hair cut short—a relief, I think, since the baby pulls it out all the time anyway. I ask my friend repeatedly whether or not it suits me, feel depressed, burst into tears. I look at my shorn head in the mirror, and recall the last time I had such short hair: I thought I looked like Mia Farrow. On that occasion, I had cut it to annoy Him, to feel the pleasure of rebelling against Him. It is my hair, I said, when He told me I should never cut it. At the same time I began to gain weight and to dress sloppily, hoping to repel Him. For some time I felt pleased, in control, delightfully and safely unattractive. His curses were my cries of freedom. I was relieved that my strategy was working; often my bedroom door remained shut all night after I closed it. Now I am filled with horror at these memories. Like thunder on a hot August evening, the truth cracks the stillness of the moment. He merely shifted his attention to my little sister. I cry for her now, the picture comes back clearly of her sitting on his lap, as he squeaks back into the black naugahide recliner, stroking her long blond hair, wrapping the curls around His finger. Like Daniel, my curls shorn for strength. I may as well have transferred the clippings to her little sacrificial head. I choke and cry uncontrollably, mourning for her. *I will lay down my life for thy sake.*

After this birth, I have a round belly where I was flat and taut before. I feel like I am still pregnant when I look at myself in the mirror, that there is still someone inside trying to get out. She is a little child, a small voice, and I must let Her out. Sometimes I hate Her so much, I refuse to acknowledge Her existence. But She is adamant, kicks me from inside, demands recognition.

Giving birth is an eruption of memory, an explosion of time, resurrection of lost souls. If I can keep this channel open long enough afterwards, the details will return. I can hear the floorboards creaking, the bathroom door closing, the medicine cabinet snapping shut. I do not want to hear any more. *Stay open, listen, hear.* Submission to the details. Recall the smell of Crest toothpaste on His breath, barely masking the smell of sour wine. The greasy Nivea on His cheeks, the bristles poking through. The same Nivea you spread on my face every night, Maman, the intensity of that scent. The sounds of His footsteps on the hall stairs, the creaking and shuddering of bones being strained, the wood beneath the well-worn carpet shuddering in after-shock, stooped like a broken back. Curly hair, long, straggly, overgrown eyebrow hairs shooting off in all directions like fireworks. I cannot write, only feel paralyzed by these enveloping smells and sensations. I still breathe it, smell it, hear it, choke on it. None of this is of my choosing.

His skin is like a snake's, cold and hairless, dry. Now it becomes clear to me why I am in constant horror of my skin becoming too dry, spend lavish amounts of money on handcream. I know I chose the man I married because he is hairy, a gentle teddy bear, warm bearded friend. I chant his name over and over when I hold him to me, chasing ghosts away. Every night I sleep with clenched fists, knees drawn against my womb, arms wrapped protectively around my breasts like a strait-jacket.

167

At a restaurant, I dream of throwing a cup of coffee at the wall; it turns into blood slowly dripping down the wall. There are pubic hairs in my food.

I daydream while staring out the window: the autumn leaves are dripping with blood, everything is on fire again. The Sacred Heart drips blood on my forehead at night. The trees are heavy with the scent of myrrh, rich autumn incense falls with the gentle rain to the place below. In my private place below there is also the steady drip of a recurring yeast infection.

I cannot eat ice cream anymore. It makes me think of long country drives when something happened to me; it tastes of guilt and foreboding. An undeserved reward for something I did. I eat ice cream today, haunted by the usual sensation of inexplicable guilt, and I begin gagging. By nightfall, it becomes clear to me what it is about ice cream that nauseates me. The way he used maple walnut or orange pineapple to help me forget the taste of his crimes. *Daddy has a special treat for you for being such a good girl.* Sex and chocolate mint forever muddled in my memory.

Every time a white car the same model as His passes by, my thighs tremble, I feel aroused and guilty and terribly angry.

For weeks there has been a tick at the edge of my eye lid; it will not stop fluttering. I wake up in the morning thinking that sleep will have erased it, calmed the nerves beneath the eye. After my first cup of tea the annoying flicker returns. Just before waking one morning, I dream of being slapped across the face by a leather strap, the tip of a belt buckle stinging the corner of my eye. When I get up that morning, the tick has disappeared. She is there again, inside me. She sends me signals, my body's coded messages, even when my mind is not willing to listen to Her.

I am overeating again. I keep hearing Red's voice, She is angry, guilty, wants me to scream. I force Her back down inside of me, fill my stomach up so She cannot emerge or scream when it would not be appropriate. She wants to get nurtured, let Her stuff Herself! She is telling me to recall the texture of snakeskin.

I am programmed to respond to touch.  The accidental and well-intentioned hand on my shoulder makes me recoil in dread because Myrrha knows that this leads to sex.  An arm around me means He will grasp my breasts next.  Only by analysing these hypersensitive reactions do I begin to unravel the clues.  And the chanting continues in my brain. *You are ugly.  No one will like you if they see you as you really are.*

I can command the respect of neither my students nor my babysitter because I identify with everyone, do not want to oppress anyone.  I have been downtrodden and empathize too fiercely.  I am responsible for all misery.

170

I want to be like other women, but I am different. Afraid to let them too close, or they will take what little of me is left. Distrustful of instant intimacy, wary of others trying to control me when I so desperately seek to be in control myself. Once I told a woman about my first child, how I became pregnant by Him, when I was a child myself. Her only response was, But didn't you know anything about birth control? I am protective, competitive, on guard.

He is no longer my god.
He is no longer my grandfather.
He is no longer my father.
He is no longer my doctor.

Those rights have been forfeited.

With no one above me, I am stronger.

Getting better does not mean feeling better; in fact I feel worse than ever, explosive. At first I breathe slowly. I am learning to say my name. I am learning that I am sane. I am opening, a flower in spring, breathing freely. I will speak. I am on the other side of the closet.

I invite a man to dinner. I tell him about my past, want to trust him. I have spent the entire day cooking a lavish French meal, want him to notice, praise me. He eats without relish, too quickly, not savouring every morsel. Probably the same in bed, I conclude. After dinner, over cognac, he looks at me squarely. *Now I understand why you are such a rabid feminist. If none of this had happened to you, you would have nothing to complain about. Why do you blame men? Look around you, most women are very content with their lot in life. That kind of trauma rarely happens. Why can't you just forget about it and enjoy being a woman?* Inside me She wants to scream. The beautiful French food sits heavily in my stomach, undigested, leaden. The anger is red, molten lava.

I am tired tonight, Maman. Tired of being just a human Bandaid, trying to provide unconditional love. I am not capable of more, cannot shield you any longer. The wound is festering.

*We wilted her. We would like you to keep your promise, Sir.*

I am friends with my boss and his wife, a couple much older than me. The man teaches me several computer languages. He and I debate fiercely; I enjoy the intellectual banter. I trust them both with my secret one night, after we have shared several bottles of wine. They turn it on me, judge me harshly. Refuse to take me seriously, attribute my feminism to a behavioural problem, a regrettable overreaction. One day it occurs to me that he is just like my father, and I am always trying to prove something to him. His wife is cold and untrustworthy, just like you, Maman, even the same age. This realization hits me like a tidal wave. Some deeper pattern here, a replay of early emotions. I stop being close. Set up boundaries. *Good fences make good neighbours.*

While I go jogging, I leave my daughter with a neighbour downstairs, a woman I have known for several months. I have been alone with the baby for days, and need a break. When I return, there is someone different playing with my daughter on the floor, the woman's boyfriend; she had to leave suddenly and left him in charge. I panic; he has the same eyes. He is too interested in the baby. I have a difficult time forgiving myself for making a mistake. What if it happens all over again to my daughter?

(Click your heel three times.)

There is no place like home.

There is no place like home.

There is no place like home.

This goddam flood of unending nightmares. The disease I have contracted is incapacitating, permanent in its devastation, and has destroyed my immune system, my ability to resist being continually attacked, reliving the pain as each raw wound is opened, or reactivated by hypersensitivity.

My friend recalls being abused as a child by her uncle. Her sister was also raped by him. Both women, although intelligent professionals, refuse to say anything to their mother about her brother, even though he is obviously abusing his own children, one of whom refuses to speak at the age of four. It is silence and complacency and fear that keeps our hearts locked away from each other. Statistics: One in three. Each has her own tale of abuse, each has a different way of remembering. The little girl inside is telling us to speak up.

When one woman speaks her story, she sparks a memory or a flashback for someone else. I envision a smoldering fire gradually consuming the air, burning from coast to coast.

There are many landscapes in my dreams that I visit over and over again. One is a long scream inside an elevator shaft where I keep falling and falling, but I can never hit the ground. I often see long country roads, stretched out to the horizon, pulled neatly together by telephone poles like clothespins, miles and miles of golden wheat, the stubble of old corn stalks hauntingly familiar, a texture that fills me with nausea. I am afraid of this territory, although it makes no sense to be afraid. I wake up breathless and screaming, dreaming of five o'clock shadows, the falling of night.

Follow the yellow brick road. The dream pictures come dark and sinister. Simple stories, but they disturb me for the entirety of the next day. You come to me slowly, Maman, and apologize for going to VietNam for two years. *It was for your own sake.* You tell me that in the combat zone you had trouble adjusting to your new contact lenses. None of this makes any sense to me upon awakening, since you have never worn contact lenses.

I miss you, Maman. A friend comments today on her astonishment that she arranges all the utensils in the kitchen drawer as her mother did, sets the table the same way, unconsciously repeating learned patterns. Another woman agrees, and all the women around the table start laughing. I do not know how you arranged it all, have no idea how you ordered your life.

Everything is reduced to the taste of chlorine; it defines all it comes into contact with, the evenly masked pretense of cleanliness. Under the water I imagine that nothing exists, that life is a liquid and slow-moving dream. I can drown out voices. Angry noises are reduced to gurgling as I glide along the bottom of the pool. My muscles stretch powerfully beneath me, I swim toward a distant shore and I have only a short time to reach it.

I dream of swimming through the clouds. I am trying to drown myself, but my body refuses to sink. Instead I pull myself underwater, find paths through seaweed. I am the little mermaid looking for the witch to pierce my tail with pearls. How often you have told me that story, Maman, stressing that it takes so much pain to look beautiful. But at the end of the tunnel I see my daughter, not the witch. I tow her back to shore. I hold her upside down by the side of the dock and shake her furiously until seaweed falls from her mouth. I know then that she will survive. I peel away the layers of anger like an onion skin, my eyes watering. Inside the onion is only a soft brown useless mush. Red's voice is fading, and I am afraid that there will be no one to replace her.

For three months, I rise at four in the morning, make a pot of tea, and try to write. For three months, I do nothing but cry. The illusions fall away: the cherished notion that you once loved me, that I had a real family, that you will come back to me one day. Nothing but a vacuum. Sadness underneath, unbearable rejection and resignation. One night the weight will lift from my body, the Lady in Blue will lift it up to heaven and I will be released.

Just when I believe that I have remembered all that I need to know, I begin to have flashbacks about my grandfather. I am so overwhelmed that I deny it for several weeks, until She wakes me up to tell me that She is not lying. Then I remember the keilbossa, the pizza, the Ritz crackers. Rewards spread out like bait on His kitchen table. The taste remains in my mouth for days. Frantically I eat nothing but cheese and crackers for several days, trying to remember by following the trail of crumbs. Compulsively I try to fit the pieces together. It is connected with the passageway and its hidden stairs.

white lies (for my mother)

I do what I have always done best, write letters that I will show to no one. In the back of my mind I am hoping that you will discover them, Maman, the way you found my diaries and guessed that I would try to kill myself. My friend tells me that when I describe my raw pain to her, I have a detached voice and nervous laugh. As if it happened to someone else.

You continue to send me saccharine Hallmark greeting cards on my birthday, addressed to Mrs._____, knowing I find that title repugnant. Your cloying messages are always correct in form. *Love always, Maman.* As if the words were yours. And I return the formalized card on specified occasions, doing the right thing is very important, or you will think that I do not love you. Some days I think it would be easier to have no contact at all.

I dream that we are travelling. It is raining, and there is only one hotel in the distance. We must sleep in separate rooms. I cannot bear to be apart from the only one I have let into my life, the one whom I love so well.

I want to be normal, want to enjoy going to parties, instead of remaining the lone wolf, afraid of someone finding out I am an impostor with no history. I want a strong woman friend, but I am not sure whom to trust. Vacillate between indiscriminate trust and overcautious paranoia. *See, I told you, it is impossible to trust anyone.* The moment I perceive some slight transgression. I channel my creative energy into creating the perfect cake, sewing the perfect baby clothes, but no one appreciates this, no one notices how much work I put into creating an atmosphere at dinner parties. I need to be alone, need other people.

On the C.B.C. radio programme, there are stories of sexually abused boys in a Newfoundland orphanage. It takes a long time for me to recognize that what happened to me also happened to them. It never occurred to me that boys might suffer this too. All my life it has seemed obvious that women were the victims. Flashback: my grandmother showing me a picture of him as a young boy, curly hair, teased for looking like a girl each time she took him out in the perambulator. Later an altar boy in the church. And of course his Father. *By the fruit shall ye know the tree.* Now the focus shifts, faint glimmering of forgiveness, sorrow. I feel released. Conversely, my anger toward you, Maman, explodes.

My friend observes that I have been wearing black every day she has seen me for the past two months. I realize with surprise that she is right; generally I wear bright, primary colours. You look like a Mediterranean widow, you must be in mourning, she jokes. I think about this later. I realize I am mourning the loss of you in my life, Maman. I am finally putting that long-held hope to rest. For years I clung to the illusion that you would one day come to me, say you loved me but had been trapped. I could have forgiven you then. Another white lie.

There is irony in my survival:  the same tools which allowed me to live through this, the emotional skills, the dissociative defences, are the very extremes that made me special to him, precisely those talents which he cultivated in me at such a young age.  My ingenuity, my intuition, my strength and courage—all a mixed blessing from my father the salesman.  When Kassandra spit back the gift of prophecy at Apollo, it would seem she kept a little tucked in her mouth, tongue in cheek, just in case.  This is not gratitude, this is making the best of circumstances.  Surviving by any means possible.

187

There is still one recurring nightmare: I am standing inside the entrance to a hospital and a woman is being wheeled past me on a stretcher. I do not know who she is, think she looks a little like me. The eyes are closed, the body is covered by a white sheet. The nurse who is rolling the stretcher by rolls her eyes too. *She is always getting raped.* I am angry at you, Maman, I recognize your face on the stretcher now, show you a piece of waxed paper that I have held tightly in my hand, open it to reveal ground cinnamon, nutmeg, black pepper, which I force you to smell. You have to remember! Your eyes open, terrified, your face is bloated and flushed a deep purple, distorted as though someone were choking you. *Promise not to tell Him, you must forgive Him, He knows not what He does.* After I pledge my silence, you continue: *Every time He does it, He holds a knife at my throat.* Here the nightmare ends because I force myself to wake up, but not before the face on the stretcher becomes my own. What is it you were trying to tell me, Maman? The dream closes with blinding white fluorescent lights, flashing steel blades, ice trapped in glass like a glossy magazine advertisement for whisky. Somehow this is connected to the glint of polar bear eyes. What does the knife mean? Is it literal? I will accept any sign from you, just promise that you will come back to speak to me again.

I am St. Christopher, carrying the heavy burden of my mother, the wounded child, the slow learner, the disfigured baby. You are my damaged child, Maman, the deformed creature I gave birth to, the unwanted and unloved baby in white sheets that rises from an unbaptized grave to accuse me in my dreams.

I dream of trying to nurse my child but my nipples are cracked like clay, bleeding, dry. In the dream I have become you, Maman, explaining to me as a child why you could never nurse me, that you were sucked dry.

In those small hours of the morning, nursing my daughter comes as a shock. The sensation of the milk letting down, recalling steel hands clasping my breasts. I always think he has snuck up from behind me again. My shoulders slope forward automatically in the posture of defense. *Do not touch me.*

189

*Hail Mary, full of grace, and if the only fruit of thy womb be this bleeding pomegranate?*

We are going home. I am discharged, and I smile at my daughter. The man in white says he must keep the notebooks in his files, even after I leave. But this book has become the only voice I have now. In occupational therapy, I have woven a twine chair seat around a pine frame. I am sending it to you now; there is a message woven into it, if you look at it carefully. I collect all my belongings in a plastic bag, and walk out into the shock of cold winter air once more.

And now that I have seen what lies at the end of that tunnel, Maman, it is not enough to wring my hands and camouflage the horror. Then turn and walk away from the jungle of my heart. Evoe! I would have you cry in recognition when you receive my woven message, but you no longer see clearly, you cannot read in code. The messenger bird has been sent back to me, its wings clipped. If only I could unwind all the strands that bound us together.

I no longer care about him, nothing can shock me any more. Beneath the horror only this terrible empty sadness, this longing for your hands. The sense of betrayal, the regret at never having known you, the opportunities missed. How I wish I could turn around now to see you watching me leave. I am waiting for you still, an unknown stranger. And if by chance your hands should reach for me at the centre of the earth . . .

193

Outside the walls of the hospital, the winter sky is whiter than I remember it. I take long walks, and the branches of trees are dark skeletons against the snow. Freud was wrong: there is nothing taboo about incest. The only taboo is public discussion of incest. All I ever repressed was trauma, not desire; I never desired for any of this to happen, but my inner child did not know how to resist, was taught not to hurt peoples' feelings. And the wound I feel at your absence is greater than any wound from him. I ache for your flesh more intensely than the flesh of an absent lover. The memory of love pierces my flesh like a thorn.

He took my body when I was changing into a woman: into you, out of you. I cannot forgive. I became the part of you which you have always feared the most. You have blamed me for my pain as you have blamed yourself for your inability to mother. You taught me how to be a victim.

To call myself a survivor implies I have power. Power with its limitations. By the milk of my mother, I will muster all I can. *Show them who is boss here.*

He used you as a shock absorber, Maman. All the times I was screaming and yelling at you, I was directing my anger at him. I could never comprehend the way you just stood there and accepted his orders, the way your head bowed low when he raised his voice.

What harm can befall me now? All of the colours are melting into pastel shades, losing their intensity. Blue reigns supreme. She gives me the gift of myself, a dialogue with all the separate parts of my body. I look at my naked self in the mirror and see my flesh whole for the first time, a stranger to my eyes. Not severed limbs and parts, but a complete image. A miracle: the mirror did not disintegrate into a thousand slivers. My vision has thawed and I see lucidly what it means to be alive. I am learning the pleasures of taking risks, learning to trust in myself.

She shifts my focus ever so subtly, so that I can see that all Her parts have always lived together, coordinating each other's movements. Confronting all of my fractured characters has brought me to the world behind the closet door. Red is angry still, Green is in pain, Blue is peaceful. They console one another. My contempt for those straight ones on the normal side gave me a sense of power, defiance, rebellious glory. But now I understand that everyone over there is crippled, incomplete. We are all looking for Oz to give us new hearts.

Half-woman, half-child.  Always on the brink.  The shadow of the valley, while longing for the mountain.  But look!  I am creating BOUNDARIES, drawing lines around the windows, painting them bright colours.  I am taking sewing lessons, reconstructing garments I have not worn for years, taking them apart because the fabric is still good, but making them over in my own style.  I am learning the things that mothers teach their daughters.  There are women out there who are willing to teach me.  I enjoy cooking again, even just for myself.  I desire it.  I deserve it.  I have many new mothers.  Every day I do something nice for my body:  have a bath, paint my toenails, play sports, ask for a massage.

Healing hands.  Feel it, shape it.

This is my body.  I take it into my own hands.

I am Ezekiel, mouth full of fire, brave fire eater. Red's strong anger surges through my veins, and I walk the streets without fear. *Liar, liar, your pants are on fire. Hang them on the telephone wire.* I am a salamander, indestructible flesh, bleeding and torn. But I pull myself together. Every time a big white Oldsmobile passes me on the street, the same make as his vehicle, my thighs begin to tremble, I feel shame at the pleasure that rises through me like an electrical current. Following the shock, I feel sick to my stomach. But I keep walking, and eventually, the sensation passes. The shame is diminishing now. Soon I will be able to feel nothing at all when that oversized white Detroit dinosaur passes me again.

I take a childhood friend with me into my dreams now. Someone who is tall, strong, gentle, a guardian spirit. When the dream is too frightening, the spirit pulls me back; at other times we confront the demons together, fearlessly, with a passion for clarity. Just before I fall asleep, I meditate upon the face of the one I want to accompany me on my night journey. In my dreams, I can now make it all the way up the stairs, and I turn on the light in the passageway. I still do not know what is waiting for me at the top.

I am afraid of losing too much weight because it reminds me of when I did not have enough to eat, how cold and thin I felt lying in bed at night. A little plumpness is like a security blanket. I cannot throw old toothpaste tubes out; like you, Maman, I scrape the insides with razor blades. All your wartime economies become habits I cannot shake. I am afraid of writing now because you told me not to waste paper; I use both sides of every sheet, leave no gaps. Poverty makes me ration inspiration, hoard my thoughts, pretend they are random scraps. But gradually I allow my writing to flow on large coloured pads, use as much as I need to fill in the gaps, put the pieces together.

I pass a doll shop, in a hurry to get home, when I see the stuffed bear grinning at me from the window with its laconic eyes. It is the same German-made bear I had as a child, but the stuffing is not falling out of its legs like the one I remember. In a daze, I purchase it, telling myself I will surprise my daughter Kassandra, responding only mechanically to the saleswoman. It is not until I arrive home that I begin to cry, the tears choking out hot and salty. I find myself clinging to this bear. I think I really bought it for myself, the idea of something not yet worn out.

I think of roses blooming, but their redness is the spilled blood of all that came between us, all that could have been, the withholding of your final blossom, withered before opening. I have a strong fear of not being able to protect my daughter. I will either raise her to be too tough and indifferent or I will be overprotective. How can I guarantee that she does not inherit the self-loathing that was your only legacy to me?

My baby awakens me in the middle of the night, caressing my arms and neck, nuzzling against my breast. This is the touch I always wanted from you, Maman, to be held so close I might know the rhythm of your breathing, know that you were alive, the heart's warm thunder, the blessing of gentle rain beating its timpani on the roof. To feel the heart thaw, the little piece of glass dislodged.
*Let no man put asunder.*

I confront you with the truth: a baby cannot reject her own mother, as you claim I rejected you. Our very last telephone conversation ends with your claiming that you would die for me. Perhaps you already have. Perhaps it is merely another lie you have spun to comfort yourself.

I have to resist the continual desire to call you on the telephone and yell at you. It is hard to stop searching the mailbox in hope of finding an envelope with your scrawl, hard not to imagine that you might really call me on my birthday one of these years, or remember who my daughter is. But I must stop these vain hopes, be realistic. I fantasize the telephone scenario, anticipating blame. I will listen to your frantic ravings, then ask—
   Who is this?
   *This is your mother speaking.*
   You must be mistaken, I have never had a mother.

But would I even recognize your voice?

w h i t e    l i e s    ( f o r    m y    m o t h e r )

For two years, no word from you. Then this tape in the mail, ostensibly a birthday gift. My sadness for your misguidedness increases when I listen to it. A self-help message, designed to help you heal yourself, the package says. *All of the things which have happened to you in this lifetime are of your own creation. Even hurtful things are caused by violence you have perpetrated in a former lifetime. Therefore accept all experiences which come your way as those of your own choosing. Remember that by your actions, you have invited them into your life, attracted them by your previous choices. Nothing that happens to you is anyone else's fault but your own. Learn to accept responsibility for all of your actions; nothing happens to you without some justifiable reason.* Maman, how desperately you seek absolution, how you cast about in vain to find something on which to pin the blame. But I will listen to you no more.

In truth I never want to see you again, Maman. Or at least I want to see you only as my heart has idealized you, more perfect illusion. My rage consumes me, burns me from the inside. No more tacky greeting cards, no more hypocrisy, no more false gratitude. No more hand-me-downs, clothing you would not even give to the Sally Ann, accompanied by your expectation of gratitude.

I donate everything that reminds me of you to charity.

I will make up my own rituals in place of the traditions you never gave me, Maman. I will pretend that my recipe has come down through four generations. Now that I enjoy cooking I no longer feel guilty that I will become merely a slave, a cook, a housewife like you; I am doing this by choice and not because it defines me. I will tell my daughter that this is how we do things in our family because we have always done it that way. I have made a new family, created a new history, I will invent a family crest and motto. I may have six children, start my own dynasty. I will collect rare china for my daughter, tell her it has been in my family for generations. You always used margarine, and I despised its ersatz taste, especially in baking. When I saw the sadhus in India sculpting from butter, amidst the squalor and the poverty of that mysterious landscape, it became too delicious a spiritual symbol to ignore. As a gesture of defiance, I will never again use margarine, no matter how impecunious my circumstances.

I dream of saving a child from drowning: Adonis incarnate. I see his face in the water and I rescue him, pull him over the side of the dock. I feel triumphant.

*What is it?*

Once upon a time, there was a very hideous modern office building I passed every day on my way to work. It was impersonal in its ugliness, sinister. In my darker moments, I often wished someone would put it out of its misery, turn out the light behind its windows, blinkered like sunken eyes. But somehow it became a landmark for me, reassuring in the very tenacity of its repulsiveness, its loathsome familiarity. I never noticed it anymore until the day it was gone, as if some assassin had read my dreams and fulfilled my fantasy of destruction. I never even had to push the detonator; the work crew obliterated it overnight, pulverized my terror, altered memory itself. I merely stood there and observed the fallout, bore witness to the rubble that marked the downfall of something I once considered immutable, permanently erected in the landscape of my nightmares. I did not actively seek vengeance, just waited and watched while the devastation of all that has ever haunted me took place, the crumbling of the lies.

In my dream I am assaulted by two strange men. I am both the girl being raped in the back seat of the car and her double who is watching everything from the front seat. The girl in the front seat calms the one in the back. There is no real experience of pain; something remains inviolable, intact. No one can take what is yours only. Her voice is serene and wise. The two men begin to weep, admit they are ashamed. She suggests a shamanistic ritual where the community will shame the two men through an elaborate ceremony. I wake up from the dream feeling peaceful.

I wait. I observe. All truth is simple. I vow to participate only in what gives me joy. The universe will provide when I am prepared to make my choice. I begin to understand synchronicity. A new kind of time, nothing like the past accounts, organized schedules of appearance. No five-year plans. I always receive what I need, when I need it; circumstances align themselves to manifest some larger reality. I need hunger for nothing. She is strong, unlike you, Maman. Her love in unconditional, no strings attached. Some person enters my life opportunely, a book falls mysteriously into my hands, ripe with secret messages from Her. Unbidden gifts, unspoken promises of safety. Often I never realize until later that I have been given precisely what I needed, though I was looking for something else. My daughter is a gift, a creation of my own making this time, both mine and not mine.

The striped stockings of the wicked witch are now trapped under the frame of the flying house, and the little people are ecstatic. The Cowardly Lion already had courage, just did not know it. The Straw Man had a brain all along; the Tin Woodman, a heart so vibrant that whole world now hears it knocking against its metal vessel in an announcement of joy. *I am melting. Who would have thought a little girl like you could destroy all my beautiful wickedness?* Dorothy is singing again, recognizing at last that she never needed all these inadequate men, damaged goods, to help her on her journey. Even the shrink behind the curtain is a failure, another silly man pretending to have special powers. *I don't think there is anything in that black bag for me.*

My therapist tells me to stay open, to breathe, to think gentle and calm thoughts. My speech therapist tells me to relax my jaw, to keep it open and not clenched. My massage therapist tells me that I need to let my muscles open out, accept gentleness, receive instead of defend; her hands across my flesh release body memories that make me cry out in pain. But the rational understanding prompted by this pain is not revealed to me until days or weeks later. Parallel messages, unrelated sources. The patterns emerge patiently, awaiting my recognition. The child within speaks. Open, soft and gentle—Her emerging voice—it becomes my theme song, I chant it to myself as I swim lengths or go jogging. Of all the things I have detested about being a woman, that gentleness especially. I feel betrayed initially. Yet the voice persists, and it occurs to me that this new gentleness is of my own choosing. If I remain open, She will jump out of my belly and my throat and I will never be blocked again. I watch my daughter playing on the floor, no longer asking myself why I cannot play like that. Her joy is infectious, spontaneous, captures something outside of me. I let her teach me how to explore new colours.

And so I will seize the day, and wrestle with it. I am wearing green again, throat chakra, colour of spring, Daphne's leaves. The tears have turned to solid amber now; sorrow trapped in configurations of the past. Museum artifacts, frozen in distant time.

Toto, stop your barking.  We're not in Kansas anymore.

When I grow angry at your cowardice, Maman, I can speak about it now, instead of overeating and forcing it back down, converting it to self-loathing. Out for a walk by the waterfront, I see a lively white bird that circles around me. I am reminded of a similar walk I took, one week before my comprehensive examinations, pacing nervously along the shoreline to try to relieve the anxiety that comes with intense study. I was watching the seagulls take flight, and at the same time thought about what it would be like to leave the competitive world of academia behind, the world that offered a haven because it encouraged me to remain disembodied, live in my head. I felt an enormous pressure removed from my body, felt lighter and happier than I had for months. To choose my own destiny, not to be bound to institutional rules, judged by standards set by others. This seemed to me the ultimate freedom. And when I see seagulls now, I recall that moment, and I think of you, wondering if you ever felt that sensation of lightness, remembered a moment in which you actually chose your fate. You are a spirit fluttering like a bird just behind the bars of my ribcage, your rapidly beating heart pushing against my own heart, but I cannot release you without cutting myself open.

Maman, I press my ear to the chest cavities of all my lovers, anticipating the ancient rhythm of your heartbeat, but there are only faint echoes. I crave confirmation of your existence in my body. But I find only the mute pains of amputated parts, dull throbbing aches, ghost memories, shadows of imaginary love.

Maman, I have to let you go now. I am no longer content to be a spectator of my own life, merely observing my actions from a distance, calculating their effect. You could never be spontaneous, act on your own. Dare I say I am stronger for having survived? Special? I still have your vulnerability, your oversensitivity, but I refuse to let this be exploited when I am unprepared. When I feel my hands reach out to protect you again, I tell myself that you must give birth one more time to your little girl, the one who is not me. No more doubles. No surrogates. Another daughter needs her mother now. I want to learn to be a child again. The paradox must be reduced, all the voices singled into one, or I will be mired in cacophony.

The Snow Queen has been dethroned. In spite of your neglect, the ugly duckling has turned into a white swan. The little mermaid prefers her underwater realm to that other world. I have to let you go, Maman. You exist only in that widening gap between the fingertips of Michelangelo's Adam and those of his creator. *What God hath joined. Dividing the light from the darkness.*

I have reached the end of the staircase, the black hole in my dreams.

The prophesy is now fulfilled.  The clues arrive intuitively, never logically.  Pandora's box of pain reduced to an innocent box of watercolours.  Harder yet to recognize my own complicity, having allowed all those people to humiliate me.  Easier to blame the past. The irresistible solace of victimization, its seductive pull.  Distraction is a gift from my daughter, this new awareness that fear is mitigated by developing a panoramic view.  The mountains in their towering humility remind me that even protective layers acquired over millions of years can be eroded, swept away in minutes.  From my Chinese teacher comes the gift of an ideogram translating the concept of crisis: *a dangerous opportunity.*

Yes, this has been a precious Gift.

212

It is Easter Sunday. I am startled by the ringing of the telephone late at night; it is a cousin I have not heard from in many years. After we talk about general matters, she asks me if I was ever abused by any member of my family. My heart pounds furiously. She has just confronted her father, accused him publicly of sexual abuse, and remembers being raped by our grandfather. She tells me about keeping a collection of scarves, dishtowels, and ropes in her drawers for years, not understanding why she carried them from place to place, why she could not dispose of them, until she remembers how she tried to strangle herself every time after her father raped her. Now she keeps the scarves as souvenirs, safety nets. Her revelations stun me. I feel enormous relief that the secrecy has ended; I feel vindicated. But as the calls from other cousins and aunts come in over the next two weeks, I begin to experience the same severe abdominal pains, a collective suffering, and the anger rises in me again.

At night I am thrown back into violent dreams, and this time each step on the stairwell is detailed clearly. I see all the missing chinks in the cement. Cement! At last I realize that I have been remembering the basement room in my grandfather's house, not an attic. My mind camouflaging the memory to protect me again. Excitedly, I call my cousin back, and she fills in the missing pieces for me, describes the cot in the basement where she was also assaulted.

As a child, I used to dream of standing up in church, gripping the pulpit and reading out a declaration denouncing him to the entire congregation. This fantasy held me stony at the funeral of my grandfather.

I speak to all my aunts and cousins; we gather for a meeting, a very different kind of family reunion. My cousin tells me that my sisters are invited, but they claim they are normal, that if anything happened to me it is my own fault for being born cold and unfeeling, rejecting my mother, and deserving whatever I got. The anger resurges at their denial.

The women of my family hold hands. I remember the little girl who wants to stand up in church, and realize that this is my church, this is my real family. Twenty-two abused by my grandfather. Four generations of abused children. We are all healing in different ways. Aunt Claire, the eldest daughter of my grandfather, now in her sixties, has just begun to remember. She describes how he came to her house, even after she was married and "safe," and grabbed her breasts while the children watched; my cousin corroborates this story with the memory of seeing her mother attacked by our grandfather. My uncle, the eldest male, had always hidden the fact that he had entered the priesthood and re-emerged broken; now my aunt tells us how he unsuccessfully sought sanctuary from his father. Patterns replicate themselves; the web of nightmares is spun according to design. My personal history begins to make sense in a wider context.

There is warmth and affection flowing freely now that the secrecy and guardedness are gone. We have condemned our grandfather in his grave, we have ostracized fathers and uncles. No one wants anything to do with you or your family, Maman. We even make jokes about having our second annual incest reunion, about how the family that lays together, stays together. There is tremendous sadness behind these jokes, but there is also strength and hope and relief.

And the gift of prophecy.

This morning is blissfully ordinary. I lie naked and peaceful in bed, washed in the lights flowing freely from the prism that hangs in my window, the miraculous rainbow of the day unfolding, spinning slow spirals in my mind. In the garden under my window, the roses are blooming again, glistening after the night's rain. A lone robin blares its throaty song over and over. I marvel how extraordinary it is that I can at last glimpse the possibilities hidden in this mundane moment, seeing clearly what is often taken for granted. To feel the magnificent enormity of saying "nothing happening." And yet be contradicted by the peculiar circumstances and absolute details of the moment, the random intersection of light and time and space, the crumpled white sheets that smell of our sleep and our love, the dust motes in the sun, the angle of refraction from the crystal—nothing will ever occur again in this combination, in this condensation of lightness and joy that dances across my flesh in splendid colour.

Downstairs a little girl is awakening.

w h i t e   l i e s   ( f o r   m y   m o t h e r )

Printed and bound in Canada by
Best Gagné Book Manufacturers